FLEET

THE PHOTOGRAPHIC COLLECTION

FLEET

THE PHOTOGRAPHIC COLLECTION

PERCY VICKERY

SUTTON PUBLISHING LIMITED

This edition first published in 2003 by
Sutton Publishing Limited • Phoenix Mill
Thrupp • Stroud • Gloucestershire • GL5 2BU

Fleet in Old Photographs was first published in 1998 by Sutton Publishing Limited
Fleet in Old Photographs: A Second Selection was first published in 2000 by Sutton
Publishing Limited

British Library Cataloguing in Publication Data
A catalogue record for this book is available from the British Library.

ISBN 0 7509 3351 8

Crested china. These souvenirs were available in most towns and cities from the 1890s until the Second World
War. They can be found in any shape or subject with a local, county, regimental or personal coat of arms. A
variety of manufacturers including Goss, Florentine, Grafton and Arcadian produced an amazing range. The
origin of the three fir trees as Fleet's coat of arms is a mystery as the earliest known local use of this device is in
the Chamber of Trade journals of the 1920s, but much of this china is of an earlier period. The crests vary slightly
between manufacturers. No Crookham pieces are known but 'The Calthorpe Arms, Elvetham' has been seen.

CONTENTS

Part One – Fleet in Old Photographs

Part Two – Fleet: A Second Selection

PART ONE

FLEET IN OLD PHOTOGRAPHS

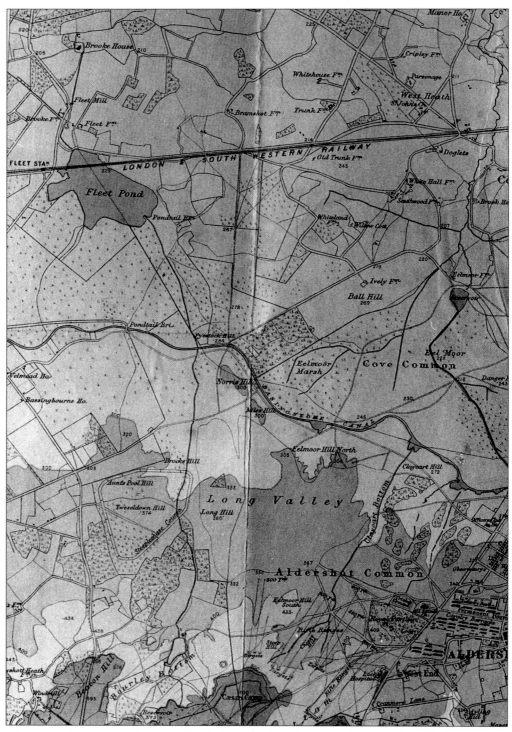

A map of the Fleet area in about 1865, showing the railway, canal and pond with a few houses and farms.

INTRODUCTION

Fleet, originally in the Hundred of Crondall, was in the Tithing of Crookham and probably derived its name from the 130 acre pond at the north end of the town, which in ancient times was known as Flete. The pond, the largest in Hampshire, was an important fishery in medieval times and was made Crown property when the army came to Aldershot in 1854. The pond became a Nature Reserve in 1972 when the large pond and surrounding area was bought by Fleet Council.

In 1505 the fishery of Fleet (the pond) and the pasture of Le Flete were leased by the Prior and Convent of St Swithin, Winchester, at a rent of 'a hundred fishes for the fishery and 23/4 [£1 3s 4d] for the pasture'; the fish were to be delivered to the priory at Winchester in good condition in Lent or between Easter and Pentecost. In 1536 a similar lease was granted for sixty years to start at the expiration of the original thirty year lease, but now instead of sending fish to Winchester a rent of 20s per annum was charged. In 1567 a 'Great Storm' caused the banks of the northern pond to be washed away and the pond drained; this left the other pond retained by the causeway (now Cove Road). To save expense, Winchester agreed that the banks need not be repaired.

The coming of the London to Southampton Railway Co. in 1847 when Fleet Pond station was opened was to have a great effect on the area, with many hundreds coming down from London to enjoy the beautiful countryside with its heather, rhododendrons and health-giving pines. In the 1850s Fleet pond was attracting crowds of naturalists who came to study the wild flowers which abounded; alas, the rarer species have long since disappeared. In the winter when the pond was invariably frozen over for several weeks special trains came from London to enable skaters to enjoy the facilities. Curling and ice hockey were also popular, with picnics being held on the islands.

Crookham Common, part of the Great Heath, was enclosed in 1834. This was the area which today is Fleet and Church Crookham down to the south and west sides of the pond. This enabled the gentry to split the area to please themselves and a few houses were built to the north of Fleet Road and along Reading Road; by 1875 the population of Fleet was less than 400.

After the Crimean War it was decided to build a hutted camp at Aldershot for 40,000 soldiers together with 25,000 acres on which to carry out training, and this land forms all of the southern boundary of Fleet and Church Crookham. In June 1878 Mr Henry Brake, an estate agent, went to an auction in Farnborough and for £2,210 he bought almost 250 acres of heathland bounded by Fleet and Reading roads, the canal and the pond which Mr Thomas Keep had acquired in 1840 as the result of the Enclosure Act of 1829. The roads were laid out on the American grid system, which was fine in those days but has caused many accidents since the motor car was invented. Public auctions were held in Fleet and London to sell the plots; at the 1882 annual land sale at the Prince of Wales forty-six lots with average frontages of 40 ft were sold at prices from £10 to £70. Crookham village became a parish in 1840 but Fleet and Church Crookham only took that step in 1861. In 1932 the village became a ward of Crondall but Fleet and Church Crookham had already become an Urban District in 1904. After much deliberation the 1974 reorganisation resulted in Hartley Wintney Rural District Council (which included Crookham village) and Fleet Urban District Council amalgamating to become Hart District. Today the population of Fleet and Crookham is 36,000, compared with about 500 in 1871.

One of the early decisions reached when the urban district was formed was to rename four roads to commemorate Queen Victoria's son the Duke of Connaught, who lived locally while GOC Aldershot Command. Later street names commemorated local benefactors and councillors such as Messrs Chinnock, Frere, Wickham, Calthorpe, Oakley, Champion, Johnson, Parsons and Campbell. Many large houses which have been demolished to make way for estates are remembered by road names such as Woodlands, Courtmoor, Stockton, Brinksway, Glebe, Kingscroft, Burnside, Peatmoor, Queen Mary, Stanton, Westbury, Dinorben, Carthonia, Darset and Greenways.

As the population of Fleet and Crookham has grown during the twentieth century so Fleet has moved to various parliamentary constituencies. Originally in the North Hants Division, Aldershot took over in the 1920s where Fleet remained until the 1970s when we were moved to the newly formed East Hampshire seat, only to be moved again when the Boundary Commission created North East Hampshire for the 1997 election. We have at times been represented by Viscount Wolmer, Oliver Lyttleton, Sir Eric Errington, Michael Mates and now James Arbutnot – all Conservatives.

The Aldershot Rural Deanery of which Fleet and Crookham are part were in the Winchester Diocese until 1927 when the new Diocese of Guildford was formed. There were only four parishes on the Hampshire border which moved over to Guildford.

CHAPTER ONE

ORIGINS

Fleet Mill House, 1912. Mrs Mallett, the miller's wife, is standing with their daughters outside their timber-framed and brick dwelling. The internal walls were wattle and daub. The house stood adjacent to the mill, but it is not known if they were built at the same time; the miller was certainly living here in 1800. The house was demolished soon after milling ceased.

Fleet Mill, 1905. Taylor's map of Hampshire (dated 1759) shows that the mill together with half-a-dozen farmhouses were the only buildings on Crookham Common, as Fleet was known at that time. Grain from the surrounding area would be brought in great quantities to the mill to be ground into flour and animal feed. The business continued until about 1940, when all milling ceased. The timber frame was removed by squatters in the 1980s, and the unsafe building was quickly demolished.

Pondtail Bridge and gas holder, 1912. The Aldershot Gas & Water Co. opened an office and showroom close to the station in 1905 when they first brought gas to Fleet. Within a few years a gas holder was built in Velmead Road to store the gas which was produced at Aldershot. In the mid-1970s, when North Sea gas was introduced, the holder became obsolete and was demolished. Houses now stand on the site.

Fleet Weir Bridge, 1908. The Basingstoke Canal was opened in 1794 and linked Basingstoke to the Wey Navigation (a distance of 37 miles) and on to the Thames. Coal, timber, flour, bricks, etc. were carried by the horse-drawn barges. This weir controlled the level of the water, allowing the surplus to be carried along a stream to the pond.

Crookham Swing Bridge, 1906. Situated between Malthouse and Poulters bridges at Zephon Common, it connected the group of cottages beside the bridge to the nearest point in Watery Lane where delivery vehicles could offload. A sack (1 cwt) of coal must have been very heavy to carry from lorry to coal shed (about 400 yards). The canal from Basingstoke to the Greywell Tunnel ceased to be navigable in the 1930s when part of the tunnel roof collapsed.

Mark Hicks. Mark lived for many years at Canal Cottage at Chequers Bridge; the cottage is believed to have been the office of the original company which opened for business in 1794. He was associated with the canal from an early age, some say when he was only ten, and he worked for various owners. When he was in his eighties Mark would work the barge horse when a barge was to be towed for a special occasion. A week before he died he was working as a canal bailiff, and his long service was recorded in the *Guinness Book of Records*.

Mark Hicks' funeral, 1966. Mark was ninety-two when he died, and in his later years his life revolved around the Chequers Inn – where he could be found most evenings recalling incidents from his earlier life for just the price of a pint. His death was marked by one of the last traditional canal funerals. Cecil North is standing in the prow of the barge while Mark's other friends, including Jim Foley and Laurie Winter, head the procession from Crookham Wharf to the coal wharf (between Malthouse and Coxheath bridges). His coffin was then taken to its resting place at Fleet cemetery.

Fleet Pond, *c.* 1910. It is believed that the 130-acre pond was man-made in Roman times; it was apparently in two halves, divided by a causeway which is now Cove Road. In 1567 the 'Great Storm' swept the area and the banks of the northern piece (by the motorway) burst and half the pond drained itself. In 1843 the pond was again divided when the railway was built between Woking and Winchfield.

Elvetham Hall, 1905. Elvetham was owned at the time of the Domesday Book by Chertsey Abbey. It passed into the ownership of the Calthorpe family in 1741 and the family have been Lords of the Manor since then. The estate stretched over Star Hill on the A30, into Winchfield and about 400 yards into what is Fleet today. Except for the railway, which cut the Fleet portion off, it is doubtful whether Calthorpe would have allowed development on his estate. The Golf, Cricket and Rifle clubs were all built on his ground and Fitzroy, Calthorpe and Gough Roads were all named after the 'squire'.

Hop picking, 1922. Hops had been grown in Crookham for at least the last 200 years as the soil was ideal. Three farms were growing the crop and at one time there were four kilns to dry them. The last remaining kiln between the green and Hitches Lane is now a listed building, and is used by several small businesses. In the last century Crookham School often recorded that children arrived late because all the family had been in the fields hop-picking since daybreak.

The White family, 1922. Grove Farm in Crookham village has been the home of the White family since the early 1890s. The 'HH' on the 7-gallon hop basket indicates that it belongs to the Howlings, who owned Cross Farm close to the green. Picking was in September and started at first light when the hops were open with the dew; they were placed in the basket just before the tallyman came along. Payment to the local families was calculated by volume. Picking was not so profitable after about 9 o'clock as the sun dried the hops and they closed up; therefore nearly twice as many were required to fill a basket.

Redfields House, 1896. Built in 1879, the house in Redfield Lane was described as a medium-sized residence standing in 20 acres. Mr Brandon bought the house and surrounding fields in 1896 and produced tobacco from 1912 until 1938. The government's 'Imperial Preference Tax', which favoured Empire growers, killed off the home trade. The house was taken over in 1940 by the War Office and was used as the Officers' Mess for the nearby RAMC Training Centre; ancillary wooden buildings were built in the grounds. The house was empty between 1971 and 1976, when it was bought by PMM as a conference and training centre. When the house again came on the market in 1995 it was bought by St Nicholas' School.

Tobacco plants at Crookham. Mr Brandon grew hops when he first arrived in 1896, but he experimented with tobacco plants until he found one which suited the soil and gave 800 lb of dried leaf to the acre, keeping eight men permanently employed. Several fields near the house were used for the plants, including the site on the corner of Redfields Lane and Ewshot Lane, where the garden centre stands today.

Harvesting tobacco at Crookham. Late summer was the time to harvest the crop; casual labour, mainly women and children, was brought in. Special carts were used as the green leaves had to be hung to prevent bruising. According to quality the leaves were either used to make Blue Pryor cigarettes or Golden Queen pipe tobacco. Some were blended with Empire leaves by H. Stevens of Salisbury to make their brands.

Tobacco drying shed. The drying/curing sheds were opposite Redfields House, where today the industrial estate stands. In the 1960s two large timbered buildings with earth floors still stood at the rear of the site; inside were a series of horizontal timbers at various heights to which the frames of hanging leaves were attached. For its last few years one of the sheds housed spares for obsolete aircraft.

Brook House, 1925. This listed house in the Crondall Road is part of a once-extensive country house with Dutch gables dated 1664. It has a later timber-framed extension. The house has been extensively restored by the present owner. According to local folklore Nell Gwynne visited Charles II here several times. Nearby Two Ponds Cottage is the oldest building in the village, believed to date from the thirteenth or fourteenth century.

Brickfield Cottages, 1918. These four cottages were sited close to the swing bridge a few yards down the lane towards Crookham Village, and no doubt housed workers from the nearby brickworks. Between Ewshot and Crookham there was a seam of clay suitable for making bricks, tiles and pots. While the canal was being constructed there was a brickworks close to Zephon Common which supplied the bricks for the nearby bridges. Brickfield Cottages and another cottage on the towpath were demolished in the 1960s.

Bridge House, 1905. This eighteenth-century house is near Chequers Bridge in the Crondall Road. The grounds were large enough to include Crookham's first cricket ground, and in the 1890s various celebrities brought teams along to challenge the locals. W.G. Grace came on at least one occasion.

The Forge House, 1905. The seventeenth-century house opposite the Black Horse in Crookham Street is a fine timber-framed and brick structure. It is probable that Mr Stevens bought the house and added the forge and ancillary buildings in the mid-nineteenth century. The shoeing, wheelwright and welding business kept Mr Stevens very busy. When Fleet started to grow just before the turn of the century he bought a piece of ground adjacent to the Hart Centre. Business carried on in The Street until the 1950s.

Crookham Road, 1901. Hope Cottages are the nearest houses on this view looking towards the Oatsheaf. Infilling and rebuilding since the 1960s has resulted in smaller gardens and twice as many houses. These houses back on to the canal, some only 6 or 7 ft from the towpath. Lea Lane is about 100 yards along on the left; you could walk a few yards and see cows and pigs at Leawood Farm. Another 100 yards or so after climbing the stile you would be on one of the public footpaths leading out to the quiet Hitches Lane.

Albany Road culvert, 1905. The stream carrying the surplus water from the canal at the weir between Reading Road and Regents Street crosses Albany Road close to the junction with Rochester Grove. During the Second World War a concrete dam was built adjacent to the bridge, enabling a supply of several thousand gallons of water to be retained for fighting fires started in bombing raids. Until the First World War this road from Fleet Road to Kings Road was called Upper Street.

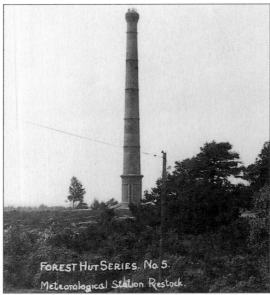

FOREST Hut SERIES. No. 5.
Meteorological Station. Restock.

Meteorological station, Pyestock, 1915. When Aldershot Camp was built in 1855 this large incinerator with its 60 ft chimney was built close to Norris Bridge to cope with the vast amount of waste coming from the camps. The army ceased to use the incinerator at the turn of the century. Various instruments were secured to the top of the chimney by the Royal Aircraft Establishment from about 1910 until 1922 for the recording of wind speeds, temperature, air purity and so on. By the time that the RAE relinquished the site the building was in danger of collapse, and it was demolished in 1930.

Oakley's Stores, *c.* 1915. These premises on the corner of Upper Street and Fleet Road grew from the original shop with house behind which opened in March 1885. Early in the 1890s the main shop with clock tower was built on the corner and Albany Lodge at the end of the site in Fleet Road, to house the growing Oakley family and some of the shop assistants. In earlier days water was provided by four wells, three under the shop and house and the other by the stable block. In 1877, before James and Clara Oakley came to Fleet, they had a shop and small cottage at Dogsmerfield. The business, Fleet's original department store, closed in 1958/9.

Fleet News office, 1902, situated close to Barclays Bank. In about 1850 Mr Morgan started printing the *News* in a 25 ft by 15 ft brick workshop, using a printing press driven by a steam engine. The *2d* paper was delivered to the local newsagents at precisely 6 o'clock on Friday evenings. On the death of Mr Morgan local businesses and the gentry were left without a printer, and in the early 1900s many of these people became shareholders of the North Hants Printing Co., which was formed using Mr Morgan's premises and press. The company remained there until 1924 when new premises were built on land to the right of Stevens' garage. The business closed in 1967.

Fleet Hospital, 1904. The hospital was opened in 1897 after Lord Calthorpe had donated the ground, and a public subscription list quickly produced £444 for the building fund which Lord Calthorpe doubled. It was decided to built two four-bed and one private ward together with the usual offices; there would be two nursing staff, matron and nurse. There were no gas, electricity or sewage systems in Fleet at this time but a water supply was laid on. Daniel Poulter won the contract to build the hospital, for £638 10s 6d. Many improvements and extensions have been made over the years, mainly by public subscription.

Ruby Cottage, 1906. This Victorian house on the corner of Albert and Upper streets came on the market at about the time the Council was inaugurated in 1904, and they bought it for the offices and a yard. The yard at the back soon had a stable and shed for the three carts; later the new (motorised) fire engine was housed in the garage attached to the house. In the 1930s larger premises were required and it was at this time that Col. Horniblow, who had always been a councillor, offered his home, The Views in Reading Road, and the Council moved its offices. In the first few months of 1936 County Commercial Cars, which had occupied their factory at 127 Albert Street since 1929 (their offices were a couple of rooms nearby) bought the old Council Office site. County eventually sold the site in 1980 to Pilgrim Miller's, the business estate agents.

Council Offices, 1953. In 1936 Col. Horniblow, having already given his grounds (now The Views playing fields, which included what today is Campbells Close) to the people of Fleet, sold the house to the Council at an advantageous price. There was much more room on this site and a large fire station with garages for the refuse vehicles, etc. was built and an area fenced off for a storage yard. In the 1960s the adjacent Harlington House and the old Ebenezer Baptist Chapel were bought to increase the number of offices as the Council's area of jurisdiction was enlarged. After the formation of Hart District Council in 1974 it was obviously not economic sense to have half the staff in Fleet and the rest in Hartley Wintney, and in 1986 the present Civic Offices were built. The old buildings and the allotment site down the hill were sold to pay for the new building.

CHAPTER TWO

EDUCATION & RELIGION

Certificate of Merit, 1890. Oliver's Charity was set up in Crondall in 1818 with a legacy to Mr Maxwell of Ewshot House from Mrs Oliver, his housekeeper, who wished her savings (£412 18s 5d) to be invested to benefit local children. The charity was regulated by an order of 1885 and initially a reward of 10s was given to those of good attendance at the local schools. The parishes of Fleet, Crookham and Crondall each received equal shares.

Dogmersfield School, 1927. The school was opened on the present site in Chatter Alley in 1911, and it can be presumed that there was a school, perhaps only a room in a house, there earlier. Miss Robinson (left) was headmistress and Miss Poulter was her assistant; there were over forty pupils between five and fourteen years old. Miss Robinson was teaching here in the 1920s and at least to the outbreak of the war, cycling to school each day from the Kings Road end of Albert Street where she lived with her sister, a teacher at Fleet School.

Crookham Infant School, 1917. The original school, which opened in 1843, was demolished in 1894 to be replaced by a larger building. The school was getting larger year by year: in 1853 there was one infant class, in 1911 two and by 1915 there were three. In 1911 Miss Chaston was promoted to Infant Headmistress and remained until 1925. Until the end of the war in 1945 the school holidays were adjusted by a week or two to allow the children to help in the harvesting of corn, hops and in earlier years tobacco.

Crookham Schools, 1958. This is the school in Gally Hill Road, built in 1911 to provide more classrooms. The original buildings were to the left of the new school and lay several yards back from the road. Education was provided here for children aged from five to fourteen years and like most schools built between the 1840s and the 1930s there were no grass play areas, just asphalt playgrounds. The toilets were located away from the school buildings, because of course when they were built there was no main drainage.

Fleet School, *c.* 1907. This no doubt was Empire Day, when the whole school celebrated together. The children stretch across Albert Street from the School House and on to the grass in front of the schoolroom. This building behind the fir tree is the only one left in Fleet where children from the C. of E. School were taught in the twentieth century. The room has in recent times been used as offices and an antique shop. The timbered house was demolished before the war and the Rose Farm Dairy now uses the site as a garage for their milk floats.

Standard V, Fleet School, 1926. The class is at the front of the school facing Albert Street. Even in 1926 there were nearly fifty in the class. Fleet's first school was opened in 1860 close to the church in a cottage which still stands today; there were about thirty pupils. By 1863 the Church had taken over the school and ran it as a Church school. By 1885 the number of children to be educated was 120, so a new school was needed. Mr Brake, who had bought a large piece of Fleet at auction in 1878, sold the Church eighteen plots on the corner of Albert Street and Church Road at half price.

Fleet School, 1926. Another class of nearly fifty is arranged towards the lower end of the girls' playground. The building behind the group was the tool, coke and cycle sheds adjoining the toilets. In 1886 only the block in Albert Street was built, and it was not until 1910 that the Church Road block was required for the Infants' School.

War shrine, C. of E. School. This Roll of Honour was erected on the wall in the top class after the First World War flags were draped either side and fresh flowers were provided by the children. On the wall in Standard V, the top class for those who passed the 'scholarship', there was another Roll of Honour listing in gold the names of all the successful students. The names of the twelve or so who passed were added each year.

School prizegiving, 1931. Billy Parsons, one of Fleet School's governors, is holding the flagpole while he gives his speech at the annual event – when the top girls and boys receive books for their achievements. This ceremony took place at the back of the main school in the playground. In 1947, when Heatherside School was built, the senior pupils moved on from Albert Street, and when Courtmoor was opened in 1960 the juniors also left, leaving the whole school to the infants. Fleet Infants opened in January 1987 in Velmead Road, and the old Fleet School finally closed; it was later demolished to make way for the houses around Old School Close. Mr Parsons ran one of his family butcher's shops in Fleet Road, close to Church Road.

Miss Pickings' School, 1926. This school used the Methodist Sunday school room in Branksomewood Road from the end of the First World War until 1933. When Miss Pickings died two sisters named Ward opened a school nearby, in the same road, and within a year or two St Nicholas' School was opened. There were only eighteen houses in the road in 1936.

St Nicholas' School, 1946. This school was established in Branksomewood Road in 1937 by Miss Pritchard and Miss McKenzie; it prospered, and by 1996 occupied several large houses along the road. Its tennis courts went through to Victoria Road. The school has now moved to Redfields House in Redfields Lane, where it is under one roof and has large playing fields.

All Saints' Church, 1921. The foundation stone was laid in 1860 by Mr Lefroy, the squire of Crondall (which included Fleet), in memory of his wife Janet, but he died in 1861 before the church was finished. It was designed in the style of an Italian basilica, cost £3,323 and was consecrated in 1862, when the Rev. William Plummer was vicar. A beautiful tomb with marble recumbent figures of Mr and Mrs Lefroy rested by the choir stalls.

The interior of All Saints', 1902. This shows how the chancel was built with the Lefroys' tomb on the left. During 1934 the church was modified and lengthened at the back, and the opportunity was taken to move the tomb to the side of the extended north aisle to make more room for the choir. In 1974 the Meeting Room was added, mainly for use by the Sunday school.

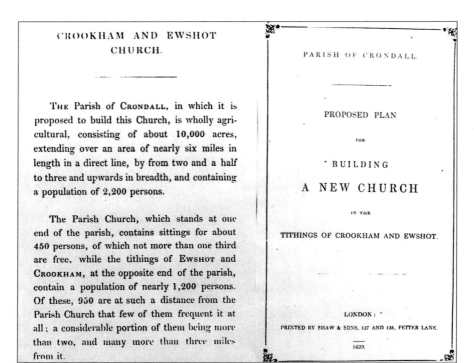

CROOKHAM AND EWSHOT CHURCH.

The Parish of CRONDALL, in which it is proposed to build this Church, is wholly agricultural, consisting of about 10,000 acres, extending over an area of nearly six miles in length in a direct line, by from two and a half to three and upwards in breadth, and containing a population of 2,200 persons.

The Parish Church, which stands at one end of the parish, contains sittings for about 450 persons, of which not more than one third are free, while the tithings of EWSHOT and CROOKHAM, at the opposite end of the parish, contain a population of nearly 1,200 persons. Of these, 950 are at such a distance from the Parish Church that few of them frequent it at all; a considerable portion of them being more than two, and many more than three miles from it.

PARISH OF CRONDALL.

PROPOSED PLAN

FOR

BUILDING

A NEW CHURCH

IN THE

TITHINGS OF CROOKHAM AND EWSHOT.

LONDON:
PRINTED BY SHAW & SONS, 137 AND 138, FETTER LANE.

1839.

Part of a booklet issued by the clergy at Crondall, setting out the need for a church at Crookham.

7

Lord CALTHORPE has kindly interested himself in the case, and has consented, with the following gentlemen, to act as a Committee to carry the above object into effect, by each of whom any subscriptions will be most thankfully received, viz.

The Rev. T. A. WARREN, *Rural Dean, South Warnboro.'*
Rev. C. DYSON, *Dogmersfield.*
Rev. W. D. HARRISON, the Vicar,
Rev. E. J. WHITE, the Curate,
Rev. A. C. LEFROY
Major BIRCH ⎫ *Crondall.*
J. A. JOHNSTON, Esq.
and
C. E. LEFROY, Esq.

THE FOLLOWING SUBSCRIPTIONS HAVE BEEN RECEIVED OR PROMISED.

	£	s.	d.
The Right Rev. the Bishop of Winchester	50	0	0
The Right Hon. Lord Calthorpe	200	0	0
The Dean and Chapter of Winchester	100	0	0
Rev. C. Dyson (from a fund at his disposal)	200	0	0
Major Birch	100	0	0
Mrs. Lefroy	100	0	0
C. E. Lefroy, Esq.	100	0	0
Rev. W. D. Harrison, Vicar (besides endowment)	25	0	0
Mrs. Waldo	15	0	0
Sir J. Richardson	10	0	0
Rev. E. Hawkins	5	0	0
Rev. T. A. Warren *Rural Dean*	5	0	0
J. Quilter, Esq.	5	5	0
W. Tillotson, Esq.	1	1	0
Rev. T. A. Maberly	1	1	0
J. Dickenson, Esq.	1	1	0
C. Richardson, Esq.	1	1	0

The committee, and subscriptions received or promised for the church. It was estimated that the church would have to seat 400 people.

Christ Church, 1920s. The church at Church Crookham was built and consecrated in 1841 by Bishop Sumner of Winchester. It also served Ewshot until 1872, when their own St Mary's Church was built. While the Rev. Gordon Wickham was vicar (1875–83) a large chancel was built; the addition included a side aisle for children's seats, which made room for more adults' seats in the transepts. The church was transferred to the newly created Diocese of Guildford in 1927.

Christ Church Mothers' Union, 1950. The Mothers' Union met in a member's sitting room in the early days, then the WI Hall by the Verne and later the Memorial Hall, until the meeting room was built in 1971. The Rev. John Langridge was the vicar in the 1950s, and on his right in this photograph is Mrs Wynne, a member for many years and a one-time leader. The banner was made locally in the early years of the twentieth century and a new central panel with Virgin and Child was made in the late 1940s.

SS Philip and James' Church, 1940. The daughter church was consecrated in 1900 to meet the needs of the growing population in the Kings Road/Pondtail area. The construction was simple and cheap, being corrugated-iron sheets on a timber frame with a wood lining; it was known to many as the iron church.

The altar, SS Philip and James' Church, just before the alterations of 1920. After the church had been standing for sixty years the timbers were rotting and beyond repair. When it was decided to build a new church, a site close to Pondtail was sought and eventually Fernhurst was chosen. In 1966 the new church with hall and car park adjacent were opened on the one site. The old church site, now P. and J. Court for elderly people, was sold after the organ and various fittings were taken up the road to the new church.

SS Philip and James' Church, 1943. The choirs of both churches were always strong and it was not until the 1950s that there were spaces available for girls. This was the choir in the days of the Rev. I.W. Moir with the choirmaster Mrs Humphries. At one time there were three generations of the Hoare family in the choir: long service was the norm in those days.

Baptist church, 1905. Built in 1893 in Fleet Road close to the Oatsheaf, this 200-seat building replaced the original Hope Chapel in Reading Road close to Hagley Road. By 1922 there was a Sunday school room behind the church, which was constructed of materials from the old Hope Chapel. This room was used as an extra classroom for Albert Street School during the war when Fleet had so many evacuees, and housed the top class. After a 1961 road widening scheme at the Oatsheaf corner the frontage was lost, so there were just a couple of steps out of the church on to the pavement. When the present church in Clarence Road was opened in 1965 the old site was sold for development.

Wesleyan Methodist church, 1910. This brick and stone church was erected on the corner of Branksomewood Road and Fleet Road in 1899 to replace a smaller 1887 wooden building on the site. A Sunday school room and kitchen with plenty of tables and several ovens and sinks were built behind the church. There were no domestic science facilities at the Albert Street School, therefore a crocodile of girls from the top two classes could be seen wending its way to Branksomewood Road every Monday morning to use the church facilities. The two Methodist churches united in 1963, with morning worship in this church and evensong in Reading Road. When the church was demolished in the late 1960s Woolworths moved in, and nearly forty years later they are still there.

'A New Primitive Methodist Chapel', 1883. The poster gives an invitation to the foundation stone-laying ceremony and tea, followed by an address in the Baptist chapel in the evening. A local publication dated 1874 mentions a Primitive Methodist church which had been built for £100, but nobody has seen another mention of this church or where it was built. This notice is for a 'new' church, perhaps more evidence that an old one existed.

Primitive Methodist church, 1921. As a result of the fund-raising events the church was consecrated in 1884 on the site of the present post office opposite Heatherside School. A Sunday school room was added in 1898 and the vestry in 1916. When the Primitive and Wesleyan wings of Methodism united the church in Fleet Road was sold, and it was decided to build a modern church by the side of the earlier Primitive church; this was opened in 1972. The new post office was then built where the old church had stood.

Opposite: Sunday school outing, 1911. Most children went to Sunday school and the summer treat for the Wesleyans was an outing to Elvetham or Dogmersfield Park, where teas were provided after games and races. The ride in a horse-drawn brake was a real treat. Later Frensham, Hindhead and Bognor were visited by charabanc. In 1938, 1939 and again for several years after the war a special train was laid on by Charlie Perrin to Bournemouth and Swanage.

Crookham war memorial, 1923. After the First World War, when the servicemen returned home, there was a rush to build memorials in the towns and villages to commemorate those who had fallen. Crookham decided on a simple cross on a stone base. Subscriptions poured in, and the war memorial was erected and unveiled in 1921 – having been made by Mardles of Fleet, stonemasons. In the late 1940s the base was modified to show the fallen in the Second World War, and it still stands on the triangle formed by the junction of Gally Hill and Gables roads close to the church.

Fleet war memorial, 1921. The memorial was originally sited at the junction of Fleet and Minley roads backing on to the Station Hotel (now Links Hotel). The Earl of Selborne, the local Member of Parliament, unveiled the memorial in April 1921. Mardles were again the stonemasons and they added the names of the fallen in the Second World War. Owing to the increase in the volume of traffic passing along the road while the Remembrance service was being held the memorial was moved in the 1970s to the library precinct, and a further move was necessary when the Civic Offices were built in 1986.

CHAPTER THREE

RETAIL

Pondtail post office, 1912. This house was built just before the turn of the twentieth century and it was a sub-post office before 1910. It is one of the last corner shops in Fleet, and is situated opposite Wood Lane.

Byrnes newsagent, 1928. Byrnes opened their business in a wooden building in 1922 in what was then Green Lane. By 1932 the hut had been replaced by the present house and shop on the same site. The road was renamed Beacon Hill Road in 1936 and the family are still running the business over seventy years on.

T.H. Mellerish and Son, 1908. Almost opposite Award Road in Gally Hill Road there were three shops: Mellerish, Dr Frere's surgery (later a bootmaker) and a butcher's. Two were converted to houses by 1937 and Mr Mellerish closed in 1938. The residents of this area must have been less than pleased when they closed, as the nearest shop then would have been half a mile away.

Jessett's Stores, 1903. This shop was on the junction of Crondall and Pilcot roads. The Jessett family opened the business in 1843 and it closed in the 1960s. Delivery vehicles (horse and carts in the early days) took the various goods to outlying areas like Crondall, Winchfield, Fleet and Elvetham. For many years Jessett's was the only shop in the village and it catered for the needs of everyone with bread, grocery, greengrocery, clothing and haberdashery – and of course it was the post office.

A. Crumplin, 1940. In 1934 Alf Crumplin built a house and shop complete with hairdressing salon on the corner of Reading Road and Albert Street. Alf with his 'boy' (Fred Godden, who must have spent forty years with Alf) started the business in a single-storey building opposite in Reading Road in 1925. In the early 1960s Alf died and his wife continued to run the shop with Fred in the salon, and business boomed when a new assistant barber was brought in – a young lady (the first female barber in Fleet). The property was compulsorily purchased for a road-widening scheme, and Fred then cycled to give clients a short back and sides in their own sitting rooms for a few years. The road widening didn't take place but the Council built Woodman Court on the site, a block of flats for single people.

Church Crookham post office, on the corner of Aldershot Road and Sandy Lane, 1936. Mr Goddard altered his house in 1908 to include a shop and sub-post office in the front room. Mr Liming, a well-known name in Church Crookham, built the house and he left his trademark, a monkey puzzle tree – which stood in the garden until a few years ago. It was removed when the junction was improved. After the war the post office closed, and today it is sited in the Verne.

E. Field, 1927. Mr Field's first shop, which he built himself, had an unusual roof line and was next to the restaurant in Reading Road opposite Glen Road. The business of 'Musical and Cycle Store' opened in 1920 and transferred along the road to almost opposite Albert Street when W.C. Baker moved out in 1935. Mr Field's old shop became a general store and was demolished by Heanes in the 1970s.

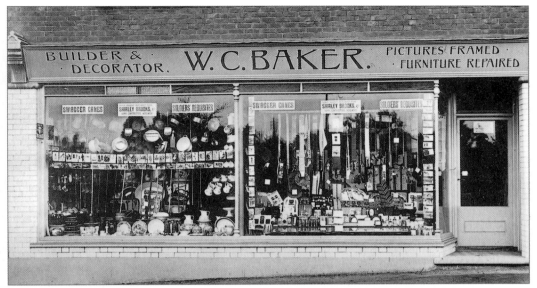

W.C. Baker, 1926. Mr Baker moved into Blenheim House in 1908 and opened a hardware shop there. In 1935 the family moved round to Fleet Road next to what is now Gurkha Square car park and built a new home and shop on part of Chernocke House grounds. Having to move out of Blenheim House before their new place was ready, they took a shop next to Lloyds Bank for a year. They occupied their new premises in 1936 and are still there today, the longest serving family business in Fleet. The shop today is run by the third and fourth generations of the Baker family.

E. Field, 1936. The cycle shop moved up the road to larger premises at Blenheim House vacated by Bakers in 1935; there was now a large showroom and more space to carry out repairs. The cycle shop remained here until 1988, by now managed by the third generation of the family, when a move was made to the end of the block of shops on the eastern corner of the Fleet and Reading roads.

F.J. Tayler, 1912. The jewellery and watch repair business spanned the period from 1908 to the 1970s on the eastern corner of Fleet and Reading roads. Between the wars F.J. retired and his son A.G. carried on the business; small boys (and bigger ones) would stand for ages at the side window and watch Mr Tayler in his workshop with his magnifying glass fixed to his eye. Originally the property stretched down to Albert Street, but in 1934 the piece on that corner was sold to Mr Crumplin for his shop, and a plot next door was sold for a bungalow.

Cane's Stores, 1930. Cane's opened in the late nineteenth century on the northern corner of Fleet and Reading roads. The salesmen would visit the homes of the gentry each morning to solicit orders for that day's delivery; delivery boys on cycles for small orders or the horse-drawn cart for bigger ones would ensure they arrived promptly. By 1930 motor vans were in use for an even faster service. The premises were demolished in the mid-1960s and the parade of shops on the corner today occupy the site of the Baptist church and Cane's.

Osmond's, 1913. In about 1906 Mr Osmond lived in a four-bedroomed house next to Mr Tayler's on the corner of Fleet and Reading roads. He foresaw that Fleet was going to grow fast, and he soon built a large single-storey shop across the front of his house. Pneumatic tyres had just been introduced and bicycles were lighter because of new technology, and sales were growing as everybody wanted a machine. The roads were not metalled and the flints caused many punctures. Mr Osmond employed a man to mend a tube while you waited. He later sold prams, high chairs and cots, and remained in business until the mid-1950s.

E. Wright, 1911. Mr Wright was related to the operator of the mill in Minley Road and he started selling animal feed from the mill to local smallholdings and stables in the district. Most houses kept chickens and many had pigs; all these householders would be customers of the corn merchant. Mr Wright, whose shop was almost opposite today's entrance road to Gurkha Square car park, had left the shop by 1920.

J. Parrott, 1912. This newsagent and tobacconist was directly opposite the entrance road to Gurkha Square car park and was trading from 1908 to 1992. Mr and Mrs Parrott owned the business from 1910 but the family sold it in the 1950s. Various people owned the paper shop until Forbuoys finally closed it.

Nelson and Goodrick, 1908. Originally this business occupied two shops, with Richardson's in between. The lower shop sold furniture while the other was a draper's; but eventually the lease on the lower shop was not renewed. The remaining shop was altered so that there were windows either side of the central walkway; the front door and shop were several yards off the pavement. The firm remained in business until the 1950s; it was a first-class department store. Shelaugh Fashions took over for several years until the area was redeveloped early in the 1960s, and a modern block with ground floor shops and two floors of offices was built opposite the Gurkha Square car park.

Richardson's, 1912. Mr and Mrs Richardson were ironmongers also selling kitchenware and garden tools, and their shop opened in 1906 next to Nelson and Goodrick, opposite what is now Gurkha Square car park. Mrs Richardson was widowed after a few years but carried on the business until 1937 when she retired.

Chernocke House, 1953. Built in the 1880s, this became the surgery and home of Fleet's first doctor, Dr Gilbert Wickham. In 1910 Dr Slade was in residence and in the 1930s Dr Greenish came here for several years. By 1939 the building was used as the Fleet Bridge Club and a couple of flats. In the 1950s the library moved from its first home, two shops down the Fleet Road. When the present library was built in 1975 Chernocke House was demolished, and Gurkha Square car park was created.

P.R. Harden and Sons, 1925. As development continued along Fleet Road, Percy Harden built this shop in 1896 with living accommodation over and a slaughterhouse at the back. He was later joined in the business by his sons Percy and Tom. When the sons took over Tom soon left the business, opening a butcher's shop in Reading Road – next door but one to Tower House on the Fleet Road corner. Eventually Percy junior's son, another Percy, went into partnership with his father, and their business flourished (as did Tom's) until the area was sold for redevelopment in the early 1960s. The large office block opposite Gurkha Square car park replaced Harden's.

Rutter's, 1907. These premises on the corner of Fleet and Victoria roads were built early in the 1890s by Mr Rutter, who saw the need for a high-class butcher in the centre of the village. The premises next door were built at about the same time but as houses; they were not converted to shops until the 1920s. The two horse chestnut trees on the pavement were planted by Mr Rutter to shade his shop over a hundred years ago.

A.L. Mill, 1932. This single-storey shop was attached to a Victorian house, Carn Brea, in Upper Street, between Albert Street and Clarence Road. The shop with workroom behind was built by Mr Mill using building blocks he made himself. The business thrived until after the war when Mr Mill retired to Hayling Island. He was a keen bandsman and belonged to the Fleet Silver Band, even lending his workroom for band practice for several years. The site is now a bungalow and car park.

Oakley's and clock tower, 1920s. The property still stands today in the main road on the junction with Upper Street, having been mainly built in the 1890s. The earliest part was an existing shop which James and Clara Oakley moved to in 1885; they then built Albany Lodge adjoining the shop. Later additions gave them the premises which today are occupied by a public house. After the Oakleys retired in 1959 the premises were variously a freezer centre, carpet and furniture stores. The striking of the clock could be heard over much of Fleet in the early days but today's chimes can be heard only a few yards away. Princess Beatrice was a customer at the turn of the century; therefore the Royal Warrant was conspicuously displayed.

Capital and Counties Bank, 1920. Opened in 1889, this was a very imposing building, with its red granite porch pillars and its stone façade. It was surrounded by trees. Within ten years Lloyds Bank had bought the premises, and in 1970 the building had a facelift – with the façade and porch being removed. The granite pillars were taken to Goddard's builder's yard for future use and were never seen again. In 1995 the Trustee Savings Bank and Lloyds merged, and early in 1998 another facelift proclaimed 'Lloyds TSB', the first joint bank in the area.

W.J. Crick, 1903. About 100 yards from the Church Road junction in Fleet Road, this shop was on the left of the old Waitrose store and was built with living accommodation above in the late 1880s. It was the first shop in Fleet to sell national newspapers; Mr Crick also had a fine stock of picture postcards of the district (this is one of his cards), stationery and tobacco. The shop changed owners several times but always held the same range of goods, but in the early 1990s the main post office closed and Forbuoys then ran the sub-post office in their shop. After a couple of years they moved along the road to larger premises.

Fleet post office, 1907. Pictured just a year after opening, this fine building is still serving the public. When the post office was closed in May 1990 the premises reopened as a building society. The first post office opened in Fleet in 1901 close to the Oatsheaf, and moved to a new shop three doors west of the purpose-built office for a couple of years.

Post office staff, 1920s. The large gas lamp to illuminate the entrance can be clearly seen. From 1906 the sorting of mail was carried out in the office at the back of the building, with the postmaster living on the first floor. As the volume of mail and the staff required increased extra accommodation was built, and the first floor was made into offices. In 1988 the sorting office was moved to the trading estate by the station, and now staff work through the night sorting incoming mail ready for the postmen to deliver.

Peter Pan, 1948. This business occupied the shop which stood 40 yards west of Church Road next to the supermarket. When Frank Bell came out of the services in 1945 he opened a sports shop, but in 1950 he moved up and across Fleet Road to a shop vacated by Mr Pace, and gradually drapery took over from sports goods. The Hart Centre north entrance stands where Peter Pan once stood. Mr Bell's original shop was demolished some years ago and was replaced by a block of shops and offices around Church Road corner.

Williams and Wright, 1968. Mr George Wright opened this shop on the Church Road and Fleet Road corner before the turn of the century, selling corn feed and flour which came from his family's Fleet Mill. He opened another shop nearer the Oatsheaf and both soon had coal pens, as this fuel had replaced peat. Herbert Williams came into the business and they concentrated on the Church Road corner site selling coal at 1s 4d a cwt (112 lb): at the time of writing 1 cwt costs £7.40. Supplies came initially by canal, being offloaded at Reading Road and the coal wharf at Crookham; the railway took over in 1900, with 10 ton trucks being delivered to the station sidings.

Rose Farm Dairy, 1906. Mark Kimber owned Rose Farm in Reading Road behind the Prince of Wales, and in 1862 began delivering milk locally. Business boomed and he built a shop and dairy in Fleet Road 100 yards past Church Road; the dairy entrance for the horse-drawn milk floats was in Church Road. By 1920 Mr Cubby together with Mr Adams from Broomhurst Farm took over the dairy, but after the war Mr Adams had died and Mr Watts from Bramshottt Farm was supplying the milk. Some years later he took over the dairy and 130 years on it is still Rose Farm Dairy. More space was required in the 1950s, and they expanded back to Albert Street. Today their electric floats are garaged in the extension.

Mid-Southern Gas and Electric Co., 1954. Built in the 1930s, the large showroom was always full of gas fires, lamps, ovens and electrical appliances. Before nationalisation in 1947 both gas and electricity were controlled by one company, with their store and workshop at the back of the showroom. During the war the appliances on display would occasionally be moved to a corner to enable a large display area to be available for the Warship or War Weapons Weeks exhibitions. The premises were vacated by the Electricity Board in 1947 but the Gas Board stayed for several years until the shops were built on the old cinema site. The electricity showrooms were almost opposite the clock tower. The foreground on the left is now Birch Parade.

Saunders' Nurseries, 1945. These nurseries fronted on to Fleet Road where an office block now stands, almost opposite Birch Avenue. The property went through to Albert Street where the frontage was almost twice as long. There were not only glasshouses but also nursery gardens. Mr T. Ayres founded the nursery in the first few years of the twentieth century and in 1923 Mr Saunders took over; the nursery stayed in his family until the late 1960s when the site was redeveloped.

H. Bracknell, 1900. Early in the 1880s Mr Bracknell built a shop opposite Birch Avenue, and was soon able to offer timber, ironmongery, carpentry and building supplies. He had a sawmill which was always busy. Power for the site was provided by three large steam engines and generators; about twenty staff were employed. In about 1904 Mr Bracknell moved to larger premises in Farnborough and Mr Brothers bought the Fleet Road shop. His ironmongery and decorating business kept several staff busy, and his son was so interested in radio and electrical goods, which were becoming more popular and less expensive, that he built an extension on the side that included a studio for television. In 1939 there were about a dozen chairs provided, and here it was that many Fleet people had their first experience of television – including Test cricket!

Avondale post office, 1920. Built in 1908 as a single-storey shop and house, Mr Chorley was the postmaster; the shop was 'open for business daily from 8 a.m. to 8 p.m.' The premises sold tobacco, confectionery and stationery, including local view cards published by Mr Chorley. A second storey was added in the 1920s, and the premises were known as the Tuck Shop until rebuilt as a specialist tyre and wheel outlet in the early 1990s. The sub-post office transferred to a shop in the middle of the Avondale Parade in 1935, and stayed there until the post office was closed in the 1980s.

T.J. Norman, 1916. Mr Willis opened the tea rooms in 1904 but at the onset of the First World War Mr Norman had taken over; he remained in business until the 1950s. From the 1930s there was a covered area at the side of the shop where you could leave your cycle for 6d when you went on the train; there were no facilities at the station for cycles. The café did a good trade from the men working on the trucks in the railway sidings. There were half a dozen coal merchants and the camp generated a lot of business.

Donoghue's Stores, 1925. This property, on the corner of Pinewood Hill and Kings Road, was built in 1905 and was a true corner shop, with a wide range of products crammed into a tiny space. After Mrs Donoghue died in 1936 the shop closed, but reopened as a café during the war; it was later a ladies' and then gents' hairdresser. The family sold the property in 1972.

Vincent's, 1909. Mr Harold Vincent built the shop on the corner of Clarence and Kings roads in 1906, together with living accommodation and stables. He came from Chertsey and established himself as a high-class butcher, in the early days selling 'no frozen meat'. He also bought an acre of land at Pondtail where he raised chickens and produced eggs. This picture, which shows Harold with his two older children, Son and Ella, shows the power of advertising: even the telegraph pole is utilised! This type of display always attracted customers before Christmas – but what would the health officials say today? Two younger sons, Leslie and Derek, took over from their father and the business remained a thriving concern until it closed in 1982.

CHAPTER FOUR

LEISURE

Skating on Fleet Pond, c. 1905. Most years up to the 1950s the pond froze over for several weeks each winter, and hundreds of people could be seen playing ice hockey or curling or just skating. Until 1929 special trains ran from London to Fleet several times a week when skating was possible. Bonfires were lit on the islands and large parties were held most evenings.

Oddfellows' Fête, *c.* 1920. Fêtes were always large events, usually for the members of the local Friendly Societies and often held in the meadow close to Woodlands by Birch Avenue. The Buffaloes, Hampshire Friendly Society, Rechabites and Oddfellows would join together, and one of the Fleet bands would lead the procession through the town. Pride of place in the procession would go to the beautiful large banners of each organisation. All societies would look after their members and their families in the event of sickness, death or unemployment – and all for a couple of pence a week.

Fishing at Malthouse Bridge, 1908. The canal, being quite weed-free after just a hundred years' use by the thousands of laden barges which had plied along its length, was ideal for fishing. Various reaches were called 'deeps', and here shoals of various species would congregate. Fishing is still very popular along the length of the canal, and small numbered discs are in evidence as peg markers for fishing matches.

Boating on the canal, 1905. Boathouses sprang up close to bridges near areas of population, with Ash Vale, Wharf, Reading Road, Chequers, Barley Mow and Colt Hill bridges being the largest nearby. Often owners of the Bridge Stores would have a small number of boats in the boathouse on the other side of Reading Road Bridge.

Boathouse, Reading Road Wharf, 1935. Various people held the licence to hire boats here over the last century but the most successful were Mr Cox and his son: they had the lease during the Second World War when hundreds of troops would hire punts, canoes and rowing boats of various types to take their girlfriends to a quiet spot.

Canal Carnival, 1926. The landlord of the Fox and Hounds close to the cemetery could always see the potential of extra trade if he organised a regatta or decorated boat festival on the canal behind the premises. This entrant shows how elaborate the entries were. Even today a couple of events a year are held at the Fox and Hounds.

Forest Hut Café, 1928. This wooden café was open at weekends during the summer, and did a good trade with rowers from Wharf and Reading Road bridges. The outbreak of war in 1939 spelled the end of this business, as the house and café were left empty and it was soon used for hand grenade practice. After the war Farnborough Airfield was fenced off, and the site of part of this property is now inside the fence.

Crookham Mummers, 1912. Boxing Day is the only day the Mummers perform, and they now give three performances – at the Chequers, the Black Horse and The Crescent. They have enacted the same play for more than 100 years, and its origins are obscure. The players, who include Bold Roamer, King George, Turkish Knight, Father Christmas and Trim Tram, wear coats and hats decorated with strips of paper.

Fleet Fanciers' Show card, 1910. Fleet Fanciers' Society held its annual show in the Pinewood Hall. The society was founded in 1904 and soon increased its interest from poultry to include cats, dogs, caged birds and rabbits.

Fleet Brownies, 1916. In their early days the Brownies met in benefactors' gardens in the summer, or when sufficient cash had been raised would move to a small hall. Mrs Slingo was their leader. Eighty years on, and the numbers of Guides, Brownies and Rainbows can be counted in their hundreds in Fleet and Crookham.

Fleet Boy Scouts, 1936. A group photograph with the District Trophy (with a wolf's head on top of the pole), which was won by the Cubs, and the President's Trophy Flag. The 22nd Odiham Group leaders were Mrs Sergeaunt (seated) and Maurice Hill. Standing are John Mill, Maurice Hill, Ray Blount and Tony Mearing. Seated are Stan Butt and Joe Standen with cubs Don Ancell, Geoff Barton, Maurice Bone and Jimmy Dove.

Summer Scout camp, Odiham, 1912. This shows the fine catering arrangements. These camps were always popular, as for most boys it was the only time that they were away from home.

Sir Seymour Hicks and Miss Ellaline Terriss, 1930s. In the early 1930s Seymour and his wife came to Fleet and bought The Courtyard in Elvetham Road. This had been the laundry of Stockton House and had remained empty after the house was sold. Seymour was knighted in 1935. During the war they entertained the troops, and remained in South Africa until 1946. They were both born in 1871. Ellaline, whose father was a sheep farmer, was born in the Falklands, but the family moved back to England where her father became a respected actor. At the age of fifteen she danced in Sinbad the Sailor with Vesta Tilley. She met Seymour, and after only eighteen days he proposed; they were married a few weeks later in 1889. Sir Seymour died in 1949 and his wife (aged 100) in 1971. They are buried in Fleet Cemetery with a white marble stone over the double grave.

Aldershot Tattoo, 1936. 'First Prince of Wales' was one of the tableaux enacted at this annual event. The tattoo started in the 1890s as a military fête and bazaar for Queen Victoria at the Royal Pavilion. In 1922 the show became the Searchlight Tattoo on Cove Common, and the next year it moved to the purpose-built Rushmoor Arena with two large grandstands seating 60,000 people; it ran for ten days with royalty present each night. The attendance exceeded half a million in 1939, but the war meant the end of the tattoos. The Aldershot Show was (and still is) held at the Arena, and in the summer thousands of OCTU and Territorials would spend their camp here.

Fleet station, 1930. Up to ten excursion trains a night would arrive at Fleet station between 7 p.m. and 9.30 p.m. on Wednesday, Friday and Saturday evenings of both weeks of the tattoo from all parts of the country: the Great Western from Wales, the LMS from Manchester and Liverpool, the LNER from York and Newcastle and the Southern from Weymouth, Exeter and so on. These trains would be met by forty or so Traction Co. buses, which quickly did the round trip to Rushmoor to keep the queue short. Hundreds of cars and charabancs would come over the station bridge, while hundreds of local people gathered at the station and along Kings Road to watch the traffic: the most Kings Road normally saw was twenty cars, one lorry and a tank each day. The tattoo brought the area noisy excitement every year – and this was duplicated in Farnborough and Aldershot.

Fleet Lido, 1949. In the early 1930s a house was built on the right of the Small Pond next to the Mission Room in Cove Road. Within a few years a public outdoor swimming pool was added behind it. Local children swam in the pond and canal with no apparent ill effects before the pool was open. Boys and girls in their last two years at Crookham and Fleet schools walked to the pool weekly between Easter and summer if it was warm enough. From 1947 (when the senior pupils had moved to Heatherside) there were very occasional lessons at the pool. Houses stand on the whole site today.

Peer Gynt, early 1930s. This performance of the once-popular operetta was given by the Crookham Women's Institute. The WI Hall in those days was in Aldershot Road where today the Verne has been built. In the latter part of the war a stick of bombs just missed the camp, landing in Sandy Lane, Aldershot Road and the last one very close to the WI Hall. The Women's Institute is still very active in Crookham, with both Church Crookham and the village having groups.

Snow White and the Seven Dwarfs, Fleet Carnival, 1938. This was the Hesters' entry, with daughter and son together with their friends. Bert Hester had a garage in Upper Street (his daughter is still a director today) and he was always a great supporter of carnivals. Before the war the carnival was held to aid the hospital, which was kept open by voluntary subscriptions. The procession started at the station and proceeded to the Oatsheaf, then down Reading Road and on to the field at Courtmoor House. Some dwellings about 30 yards back but facing Reading Road had been built at this time, but behind these there were no houses. The 1939 event was the last before the war and we had to wait until the early 1950s for the next.

Vincent's barrel organ, 1936. This was an entry in the Hospital Carnival. Each year these floats raised hundreds of pounds. Strong support for the procession was assured, as the traders were getting good publicity while supporting the cause.

Legion of Frontiersmen, 1938. The Legion was a local organisation led by Fred Liming of Reading Road. Members wore blue tunics with chainmail on the shoulders and Canadian Mountie-style hats; their horses were well trained and well turned out. The various fêtes were enhanced by the procession along Fleet Road with the banners of the Friendly Societies, and larger crowds would be drawn when the Frontiersmen also paraded. The events took place on the field near Birch Avenue, The Views or The Firs (now the police station), and the horsemen would on some occasions put on a display including tent pegging and jumping.

Fleet Youth Club, 1946. This photograph was taken at the opening of Fleet Youth Club in Kings Road Broadway by the Rt Hon. Oliver Lyttleton MP for Aldershot (which included Fleet), accompanied by Lady Crookshank. The leader of the club was Mr E.T.J. Tapp of Kings Road. The club was open most evenings, with rooms catering for snooker, table tennis, darts and drama.

Warship Week procession, 1942. The children joined the main procession at the school in Albert Street and went along Fleet Road to the Oatsheaf and down to the cricket ground. During the war various 'weeks' were organised: in 1940 the Spitfire Fund; in 1941 War Weapons and in this year Warship Week. The idea was to encourage everybody to buy Savings Certificates (15s each), thereby providing money for weapons, etc. Fleet and Crookham saved enough money to buy a corvette named *Itchen*. There was a ceremony daily during the week when the 'indicator' would be adjusted to show the total collected.

Model corvette, 1942. Built around a lorry, this boat was parked at strategic sites during Warship Week, and of course it headed the procession around the streets on the Saturday. Here the vehicle is parked in front of Dr Greenish's house, opposite today's police station.

Victory celebration tea, 1945. In spite of the strict rationing which was still in force, plenty of sandwiches and cakes were made for these parties. This one was outside Marlborough Villas in Clarence Road, a few yards from Church Road. Traffic was not a problem as very few people were running their cars: petrol rationing had not been relaxed yet.

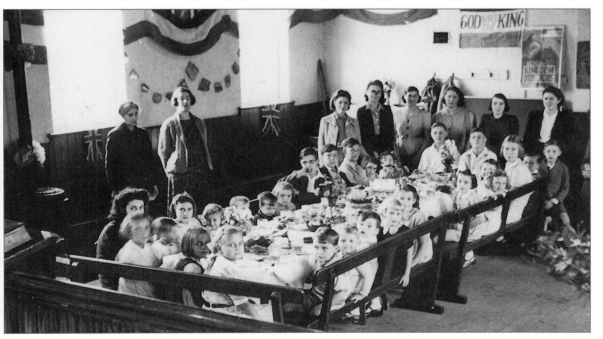

Victory celebration tea, 1945. This party for local children was held in the Salvation Army Hall in Albert Street at the junction of Reading Road. Very few children would be absent and very few parents would not help with these parties; after five years of war everybody worked together.

Fleet Carnival Band, 1958. Alex Fitzpatrick is the local lad leading the band. He had a way of enlisting his friends to dress up and entertain the public: thus began several years of the Carnival Band. He persuaded any of his friends who could play a musical instrument (or who were willing to learn) to join, and borrowed instruments from the now defunct Fleet Brass Band. Several members were trained during their time in the services and on the day they presented a balanced band, but it was also the topical uniforms that enthralled the crowds.

Fleet Carnival Band, 1964. This year they saluted Tony Hancock with the East Cheam Colonials; previously we had seen in 1958 (above) St Trinian's All Girl Band (after the film) and in 1959 the 13th Suez Canal Lancers (after the Suez invasion). Late in 1966 the Trustees sold the remaining instruments belonging to the old Fleet Brass Band, and that killed off the Carnival Band.

CHAPTER FIVE

UNIFORMS

Fleet Section Territorial Army, 1909. This group of local men met at the Gymnasium in Albert Street (now Victoria Court) twice a week for drill. Sergeant Creeper of Clarence Road was in charge. The Territorial Army was formed in 1908, and this section was previously part of E Company of the 4th Battalion Hampshire Regiment. They are shown here at camp on Salisbury Plain.

Tweseldown Racecourse, 1903. This Army steeplechase course is close to the North Horns, and various hunts hold point-to-point meetings here in the spring, while other facilities make it suitable for three-day events. When Aldershot Camp was built in 1885–6 the Queens Parade Ground at North Camp was soon used as a racecourse (flat), and Tweseldown was laid out with its jumps ready for the first event in 1867 – mainly for the cavalry. Parts of the course were used for the equestrian events in the 1948 Olympic Games.

Officers' Quarters, Ewshot Camp, 1907. The entrance to Leipzig Barracks was just past the North Horns and stretched across towards Ewshot Lane; it was the permanent home of the Royal Field Artillery. Attached to the barracks were the Quetta and Punjab married quarters. The whole site was cleared in the 1970s, and Quetta Park married quarters were rebuilt close to Ewshot Lane.

Royal Field Artillery, 1914. No doubt from Ewshot Camp, they are passing down Crookham Street to Pilcot Road. This Brigade could be on its way to Salisbury Plain for summer manoeuvres, a trip that could take several days.

Tweseldown Camp. The camp at Crookham crossroads gave a great deal of work during construction to local tradesmen and craftsmen; within a year the camp was occupied. Haig Lines, as it was later called, was the home for Hungarians who fled to Britain after the uprising in 1956. They were later dispersed to homes all over the country. Later, troops about to do their spell of duty in Northern Ireland would train in the camp for 'house search' training assisted by the Gurkhas from down the road at Queen Elizabeth Barracks.

Haig Lines, 1914. Various units used the camp during the war. The areas between the 'Lines' was grassed over, with flower beds bordered by the regulation whitewashed stones. Soldiers who offended and were 'confined to barracks' would have to spend time repainting the stones. The camp was demolished in the 1980s and was replaced by a housing estate.

Crookham crossroads, 1923. Haig Lines became the Depot of the Royal Army Medical Corps in 1915; it remained here until 1932 when they moved to Keogh Barracks, Mychett – staying there until the outbreak of the war in 1939.

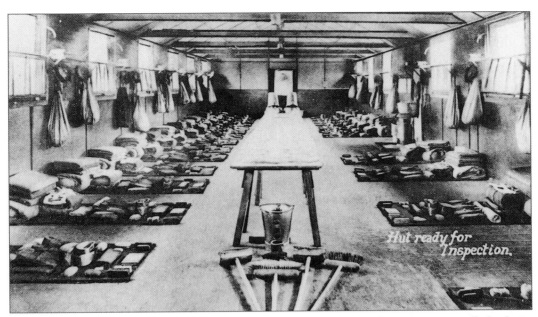

Inside a barrack room, 1915. This would be the scene at 7.45 every morning in all the huts: everything spotlessly clean, folded precisely and laid out exactly in its place. Broom handles would be scraped with a razor to keep them clean.

Miss Daniels Soldiers' Home, 1940. Marwell Lodge in Aldershot Road, near the Foresters, was rented as a Miss Daniels Home during the Second World War. Mrs Daniels was an officer's widow who in 1862 (just six years after Aldershot Camp was built) decided that soldiers should have somewhere to relax other than in a public house; so she raised funds and rented houses in areas with camps. During the last war her successors were still carrying on her work. All the homes were equipped with lecture, writing and games rooms just for soldiers.

Queen Elizabeth Barracks, 1950. This camp was built in 1938 for Militia Training (readiness for war) in Sandy Lane close to the Wyvern, with the RASC providing the staff. By 1940 the RAMC had moved back because their Mychett Barracks were now too small to train thousands of medics, and they stayed here until 1964 when they moved back to Keogh. In 1971 the Gurkhas came to Queen Elizabeth Barracks, and all of their regiments have been in residence since. They moved to Sheerness in 2000, when the last wooden-hutted camp in the country will be demolished.

Queen Elizabeth's visit, 1948. On 23 June 1948 Queen Elizabeth (now the Queen Mother) visited the RAMC at their Depot and Training Centre at Boyce Barracks, on the occasion of the Corps Golden Jubilee. The camp was named after a former GOC of the RASC, who were the first unit to use the camp. The camp became Queen Elizabeth Barracks on this day in honour of their Colonel-in-Chief. The Queen lunched with the officers at their Redfield House mess. In the afternoon she toured the Barracks, and as can be seen met the wives of some of the staff.

R. A. Horses Taking Swimming Lessons.

Horses swimming, 1906. Horses are natural swimmers but cavalry horses had to be trained to swim in pairs, with their riders and to swim from A to B; their natural tendency is to get out of the water.

Cavalry Swimming Horses, Aldershot

Cavalry Horse Pond, 1910. The 2½-acre pond was at Long Bottom close to Bourley, and here you can see the lines to which the horses were attached as they swam across. Many horses were lost over the years as thousands passed through this training, and in 1912 two soldiers who had drowned here were commemorated in St George's Garrison Church by a plaque on the wall. This area was the training ground for all of Aldershot's cavalry horses.

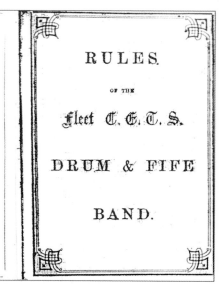

RULES.

1.—That this Band shall be called "THE FLEET CHURCH OF ENGLAND TEMPERANCE SOCIETY DRUM-AND-FIFE BAND."

2.—That each Member shall be a total abstainer, and pay a weekly subscription of 2d. to the Band Fund.

3.—That the Bandmaster shall choose the music to be played.

4.—That every Member shall attend each practise for three months after joining the Band, unless exempted by the Bandmaster as efficient; after this every Member to attend one practise weekly (unless positively prevented) or pay a fine of 2d.

5.—That no Member will be permitted to bring any friend to the practise, except to introduce him as a Member, or by permission of the Bandmaster.

6.—That anyone wishing to join the Band after April, 1886, shall pay an entrance fee of 6d., which shall include that week's contribution; and all fines and subscriptions shall go to the Band Fund.

7.—That anything bought out of the fund shall belong to the Band, and any Member leaving the Band shall return all property belonging to the Band in good condition, or pay the value thereof.

8.—That any Member leaving the Band shall forfeit all claim or share in any articles or funds of the Band.

9.—That no Member shall write his name or make any mark in his music book, without the consent of the Bandmaster; play his instrument out of turn on practise night; or play his instrument to or from the place of practise.

10.—That any Member being four weeks in arrears with his subscriptions shall receive notice to that effect, and if he shall not pay in one week shall be fined 2d., and not be allowed to practise till his fine and subscription is paid.

11.—That no smoking be allowed in the band-room, or when playing on the march. Members using obscene or indecent language will be fined 3d.

Approved by the Commitee.

T. HORNIBLOW }
H. PARNELL   } Hon. Secs.

April 1st, 1887.

RULES.

OF THE

fleet C. E. T. S.

DRUM & FIFE

BAND.

Drum and Fife Band, 1887. The Church of England Temperance Society formed this band in 1886. It was founded by Colonel Horniblow, and Mr Parnell was the bandmaster. The rules are very strict but the threat of being fined must have been a deterrent. The band was always invited to accompany the banners of the Friendly Societies on fête days.

Fleet Wesleyan Band, 1913. The band in their smart blue uniforms always paraded with the banners of the Friendly Societies on fête days. The band was based at the Wesleyan Methodist Church Hall and was formed in the early years of the century; in later years it became Fleet Brass Band.

Fleet's first fire appliance, 1905. After a disastrous fire at Richard Pool's (in the background), when several horses were killed in their stables, and a couple of serious house fires, business people demanded a fire service and in 1900 Fleet Volunteer Fire Brigade was formed. They had no pumps but Mr Pool provided a horse, cart and stable; the hoses were connected direct to the mains. Hoses and standpipe were carried in the cart and the men in their uniforms and helmets cycled to the fire. It is related that one particular horse on hearing the alarm bells would get excited and kick his stable until the crew arrived; the noise woke residents in Albert Street.

Fire escape ladder and crew, 1904. Crookham had their own Brigade under Fleet Council, with two handcarts to carry the 470 yards of hose, standpipe and the fire escape ladder. By 1910 there were eight firemen, including the foreman; unlike Fleet they had to run to the fires. The fire station was opposite the Wyvern and the siren was in Gally Hill Road.

Firemen and cart, 1904. This was the crew taken over by the Council, and some of the equipment carried in their cart is on display. By 1920 they had a Model T Ford which carried the ladder, hoses and crew; this was kept in the garage of the Council Offices adjacent to Upper Street.

Fire engine and crew, 1934. This year a Dennis engine with a built-in pump to increase the water pressure was purchased. It had increased speed and better road-holding. The engine was kept in the garage in Albert Street until 1936, when the Council moved to The Views and a new fire station was built at the end of the tree-lined drive which is now by the side of Gurkha Square car park.

Fire at Burt's and Royal Dairy, 1908. G.E. Burt's newsagent and tobacconist's shop was gutted by a fire in 1908 and the Royal Dairy next door was badly damaged. When the newsagent's shop was rebuilt it was taken over by Mr and Mrs Parrott; the Royal Dairy reopened and only closed at the outbreak of war. The shops were opposite the entrance road to Gurkha Square car park.

Fire at Parnell's stables, 1930. The wooden stables and outbuildings behind the shops opposite Gurkha Square car park were destroyed by a disastrous fire; much stock was lost when the paraffin tank split. The fire brigade prevented the flames spreading to the shops and Mr Parnell rebuilt the outbuildings in brick.

Decontamination squad, 1943. Recruitment for Civil Defence began in 1937–8 owing to the threat of war. Lt-Col. A.E.S. Fennell was appointed Controller of Civil Defence and soon the various sections were built up, some at Pool's near the station (now the business park) and others in the yard by The Views. The purpose of decontamination was to identify the type of gas being used in an air raid and to employ the correct chemical to neutralise its effect.

Home Guard, 1944. No. 5 HQ Platoon, C Coy, 25th Hampshire Battalion Home Guard were based at County Commercial Cars in Albert Street, where at least seventeen members worked. The platoon learnt many of the disciplines taught to regular soldiers, and as well as night and weekend exercises many nights were spent guarding the gasholder at Pondtail Bridge and the length of railway. Lt-Col. Fennell, who was a well-known Fleet figure, is pictured second from left in the front.

CHAPTER SIX

TRANSPORT

*White's steam engine, 1907. Grove Farm in Crookham Street used this steam engine for various tasks for
many years. Its principal uses were thrashing the corn (separating the grain from the straw), removing dead
trees and sawing logs. The belt driving the thrasher was driven by the large flywheel above the back wheel.
The family took over the farm in the 1890s and they are still in residence today.*

Steam engine and pantechnicon, 1900. Richard Pool owned the site between Fleet Road and Albert Street. A multi-storey depository and later two facing covered parking bays were built for the vehicles. Three Foden steam engines were parked at night around the corner at 127 Albert Street, a corrugated building belonging to a relative, Mr Pool of Ewshot. Half a ton of coal was always carried to 'feed' the engines, and on overnight trips the crew slept in the van. These iron horses were kept on the road until the 1920s, when parliament put a heavy road tax on them.

Horse vans, 1910. Local deliveries and removals were made by Richard Pool with these teams of vans, and the number to be seen indicates that this was a large business. By 1920 motor furniture vans were in use, with the fleet size growing to six vans and four or five tippers – mainly carrying coal and coke from the station sidings to the camps.

Motor pantechnicon, 1946. Immediately after the war this Jensen was built in the 'new' material, aluminium. The war had brought about so many developments in materials, uses and production methods that almost everything had changed. This vehicle was 30 ft long, very high and extremely light; therefore with an engine twice the horse-power of its pre-war predecessor it could carry a much larger load. In the late 1950s Richard Pool's was sold to Cantays of Basingstoke, and the site was sold.

Steam lorry, 1912. Mr Stevens ran his business from his home in Connaught Road, where Hartsleaf Close has since been built. He had a Foden steam lorry for many years and later used a petrol-engined lorry on local haulage work.

Recovery lorry with car, 1923. Ian Bradley built a garage in Fleet Road almost opposite Stockton Avenue in 1920; the showroom and office fronted the main road and access to the garage and paint shop (little more than a large garage) was from Albert Street. The recovery lorry was a Scammell with the first drop-frame trailer in Fleet. Here they had just recovered a 1921 Lanchester. The paint shop on the left of the site in Albert Street was a do it yourself business from the 1950s to the 1980s. Ian Bradley went into partnership with Mr Mathews in 1928 and they closed the business at the outbreak of war in 1939. After the war Stevens' Garage used these premises (½ mile from their garage) and Enticknap's (see p. 105, lower picture) for a few years, mainly for storage of an ex-WD contract for 100 trucks. After many years the site was cleared, and now two office blocks stand on the site.

Light Parcel Carrier, 1910. This company delivered parcels twice daily on a circuit of Fleet, Bentley, Farnham, Aldershot, Tongham, Farnborough and Cove. The vehicle was an Auto-Carrier, made by AC Cars of London between 1908 and 1912. This Aldershot-based vehicle had a yellow body and rich maroon leather seat. Richard Pool was the agent in Fleet.

Resurfacing the road, 1912. Surfacing the roads was undertaken by the Council, to reduce the complaints of dust in the summer and potholes and ruts in the winter. The tar tank was heated underneath and the liquid tar was pumped through hoses and sprayed on to the road; small chippings were scattered in the tar by shovel and the result was rolled by the steam roller. Laslett's were in the Fleet Road, in the right-hand of the pair of single-storey shops five below today's Gurkha Square car park.

Council dustcart, 1915. This was one of the first dustcarts with fitted covers to keep in the dust and smell. There were two sliding covers each side, not opposite each other. The refuse was tipped in the opening from the zinc bath that two men carried to your dustbin. Much of the rubbish was ash from coal fires, so it was a dirty, dusty job. Up to the end of the war the rubbish was tipped off Pondtail Road, and in later years it built up the common land where Tavistock was built. This view shows the rear of the Council offices from Upper Street.

Parnell's horse and van, 1922. Parnell's had several horse carts: one four-wheeled cart had a large tank to deliver paraffin (used for heating and lighting) all over the district. This van was the boot and shoe vehicle; it would travel to Hartley Wintney and on to Odiham and anywhere else they had a boot repair contract. The repaired boots and shoes would be loaded up in the morning and the van would return in the evening with footwear needing to be cobbled. Parnell's are now accepted as the earliest shop to trade in brick-built premises in Fleet Road. The shops were built in 1880 by Mr Parnell's London builders, who travelled to Fleet daily by train arriving at 7 a.m. They brought some of the lintels from Newgate Prison which they were demolishing at the time, and these were built into the upper floor.

Eales Brothers' coal lorry, 1925. Two brothers, Percy and Leonard, started the haulage firm in the early 1920s from their house in Reading Road, adjacent to St James Road; their yard was behind the house. They were soon appointed parcel agents for the Southern Railway at Fleet and were running two Ford Model T lorries. They lost the contract in 1948 with nationalisation. In the 1920s a platform Model T was purchased and a coal delivery business was built up, with the coal pens in their yard; this side of the business lasted about fifteen years. After the war Percy's three sons came into the business and the two founders retired. The haulage business closed in 1986 when one of the brothers retired.

Pool's horse brake, 1900. Richard Pool, who had a haulage and furniture removal business in Upper Street, introduced the first service for passengers to Aldershot at the turn of the century. The buses were operated as Fleet and Aldershot Omnibus Company from Pool's office near Lloyds Bank. Charlie Vickery was the driver; he expected the customers to walk up the hills on the route.

Warren's coach, 1930. In 1927 Mr Warren of Atbara Road operated Fleet Coaching Co. and he applied for a licence to run a service from Bramshott Golf Club through Fleet to Aldershot. Fleet Council approved but Aldershot refused. The Aldershot and District Co. had a licence (from Aldershot Council) for a Kings Road service. This started a price war, with the 'Traco' putting two 'chasers' on every Warren service. In two years the return fare to Aldershot dropped from 1s 3d to 3d until a frequency agreement was reached. Warren's ten Guy buses were bought out by the 'Traco' in 1936.

J. Wise's pony and trap, 1925. Mr Wise ran a pastrycook and confectionery business in Aldershot Road in the left-hand shop at Pondtail Bridge. The business ran from 1925 until the outbreak of war. He made a name for quality, and regular deliveries were made all over the district.

Mr P. Neal and milk float, 1928. Oakwood Dairy, run by Mr Neal, was in business from 1926 to the 1950s. There were half a dozen 'one man dairies' in the area in the 1930s and '40s but not many survived as long as Neal's. In the early days the cart was fitted with a large churn with a tap and ½ pint and 1 pint measures. The measure was filled from the churn and the milk was tipped into your jug. There were two deliveries a day seven days a week before the war.

Rutter's horse and cart, 1910. Rutter's, on the corner of Victoria and Fleet roads (north side), opened as a high class butcher – both in the quality of the meat and also the speed of delivery of orders to the big houses.

Rutter's errand boy, 1922. Frank Cousins started at 8.30 a.m. daily and finished at 8.30 on Saturday evening. His family lived at Ancells Farm in a tied cottage; his father was in charge of the polo grounds. Frank would make deliveries all morning to the outlying areas with the smaller packets, perhaps 3 or 4 miles away, and would then cycle home for his thirty-minute dinner break.

Fleet Coach, 1949. A new coach with Vincents of Reading bodywork was photographed at a pre-delivery trade fair. The company was founded in 1924 by the William Davieses (father and son) and they started as motor engineers. After the war W.G. Davies started the coach business and it soon became Fleet Coaches; today they run a fleet of a dozen or so luxury coaches.

Two Fleet Coaches and staff, 1955. Jack Welch, mechanic, and drivers Bobby Hunter, Ron Vimpany, Steve Sayers and Jack Rushbridge are shown. The business started in small premises between the Oatsheaf and the police station and today occupies four large garages and an office in the same area. Among the directors today are the two daughters of 'young' Bill Davies.

Fleet station approach, 1927. A Traction Company coach is waiting to start its run back to Aldershot and three taxis are parked in front of the station. A quiet scene, but if you went to the right of the coal trucks there would be a totally different picture with many men unloading the trucks either into pens (adjacent to today's business park) or on to carts; this was all done with shovels or forks, nothing mechanised. The sidings went through to the end of today's car park and there were two tracks in places. Four trains a day, two up and two down, would shunt the trucks, collect the empties and place the full ones in their correct place in the yard. The goods yard closed in 1969.

Fleet station, 1906. A fine view of the entrance to the platforms that was built when the tracks were upgraded from two to four lines in 1904. On the other side of Station Bridge, where the original Fleet Pond station had been built, there was a siding against the golf course where half a dozen coal trucks were left for the pump house, which provided air for the electro-pneumatic signal system. Air for the system between Brookwood and Worting was provided here. In the late 1950s the steam engine was changed to an electric motor but in 1966, on electrification, a new system was installed and the pump house etc. was demolished.

Fleet station, 1925. The photographer is standing on the Up platform looking towards Station Bridge with an express approaching. At the end of the platform by the bridge was the stationmaster's house; there was one at each station until the 1950s. Today the gate on to the platform can still be seen in the iron railings, while the site of the house is now part of the car park. The building on the left behind the Down platform is the parcel shed, which held three box wagons. This is where Eales Bros collected parcels for delivery around the district.

Bramshott Halt, 1950s. A Schools class locomotive is passing through the Halt on its way to Basingstoke. The Halt was opened just after the golf club started in 1905 when motor cars were not common and closed in the 1950s. In the last few years before it closed three or four trains a day would stop if a request was made in advance to Fleet or Farnborough station. In the late 1940s and '50s the army built a petrol storage facility at what was later to become Fleet Pond picnic area, and a siding was run alongside the normal lines to this area for the tanker wagons to be discharged.

CHAPTER SEVEN

SPORT

A vintage De Dion, 1930s. The Stevens brothers were in the motor business almost from the introduction of the motor car. They were often called to Ewshot Hall where Col. Wilkes had a motor car. Soon Lord Calthorpe and Dr Frere (a local GP and benefactor) bought cars from Stevens Bros. In the 1930s and '40s there was often a 1904 De Dion in the showroom; this was entered in the London to Brighton run. Here Redvers Stevens is seen with Syd Farr navigating.

Crookham Football Club, 1897. Various grounds were used by the club over the years including a site close to Coxheath Bridge, but in the 1930s they moved to Abercorn playing fields opposite the Wyvern. They joined the Aldershot League as soon as it was founded and moved up and down the divisions for many years. This team comprised E. Potter, H. Griffin, S. Griffin, ? Jenkins, ? Dempster, F. Rydon, R. Sisterton, F. Bloor, J. King, A. White, E. Simms, W. Wake and W. Goddard.

Fleet Wednesday football team, c. 1905. Until the late 1960s most shops closed at 1 p.m. on Wednesday afternoons to enable the staff to work on the other five and a half days in the week (excluding Sunday). 'Wednesday' football and cricket teams were generally made up of shop staff who could not play on Saturdays. This team, which played in the Aldershot Wednesday League, was G. Vass, H. Hodder, H. Sayers, F. Love, J. Long, H. Tocock, W. Stacey, J. Bowerman, F. Fround (captain), J. Carter and A. Oakley, with F. Parker (referee, a newsagent) and P. Harden (linesman, a butcher).

Fleet football team, 1950. After the war Fleet played in the Aldershot League at their ground in Crookham Road opposite Glen Road. In the 1960s they became more ambitious and joined the stronger Basingstoke League. This team comprised H. Pearce, D. Stacey, R. Sawyer, G. Hill, D. Powell, J. Byrne, D. Gardiner, R. Goodsell, S. Brown (captain), J. Brooks and S. Sayers. The colours from the '20s (at least) were light and dark blue.

Hunt meeting at the Oatsheaf, 1905. Mr Chinnock of Dinorben Court owned a pack of fox hounds and often brought them to the Oatsheaf for the meet. There was very little danger in having forty or so dogs and horses running along the road at this time. They invariably hunted over the Calthorpe estate.

Fleet Ladies' Hockey Team, 1928/9. The ladies' section of the Hockey Club played twenty-seven matches in this season with teams from as far away as Basingstoke, Godalming, Byfleet and Reading. Miss M. Pidwell was the captain. Matches were played on the side of the cricket field, alternating with the men's team. Dr Frere was the Club President.

Fleet Men's Hockey Team, 1927/8. The men's section played twenty-seven matches in their black and orange strip with teams from as far away as Woking and Basingstoke. The club was formed in 1925 and is still in existence today, playing on the same ground. Transport to away matches was provided by Mr Hankins with one of his covered lorries, and his invoice for all the away games in this season was for £7 13s 4d.

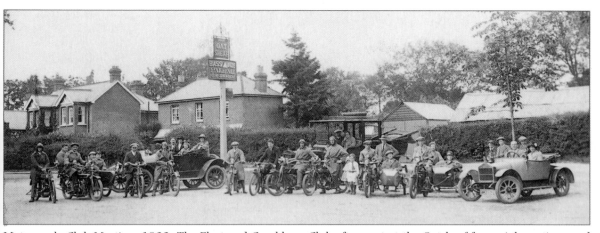

Motor-cycle Club Meeting, 1922. The Fleet and Crookham Club often met at the Oatsheaf for social meetings and when they went on a run. The machines in those days were smaller and less reliable, and the club would organise navigation and reliability runs – often at night. As can be seen there was a range of machines, solo and with sidecars, and even light cars.

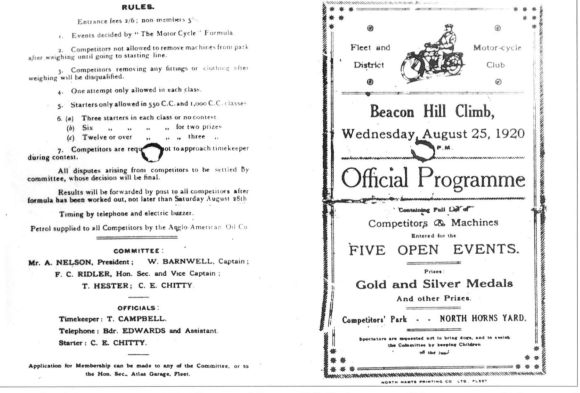

Motor-cycle Club programme, 1920. The annual Beacon Hill Climb was a well-known event which attracted entries from a wide area. The idea was to climb the hill (a rough track on Army ground) in the fastest time, and often just to get to the top was an achievement. The secretary was Mr Ridler, the one-time owner of the Atlas Garage in Fleet Road; he was building two-stroke and four-stroke motor-cycles. The other committee members were no mean riders and mechanics.

Fleet Cricket Club, 1929. Matches were played at The Beeches, owned by Mr Bloore, until he sold the property and the North Hants Golf Club was laid out. Matches were then played on the field by Birch Avenue until the Cricket Club was founded, and Lord Calthorpe gave a piece of ground in Reading Road at a cost of £5 a year. The club, founded in the first few years of this century, still plays on the same ground. The event pictured is the annual 'married versus single'.

Crookham Cricket Club, 1904. Cricket was played in Crookham near Chequers Bridge as early as the 1890s, and by the 1920s matches were played near the Wyvern; but the Fleet club with its better ground and facilities brought about the demise of the village team. The Rev. W.J. Wickham, long-time vicar of Crookham, is shown wearing a boater.

Bramshott Golf Club, 1908. Entrance to the club was opposite Bramshott Bridge off Cove Road. The course was opened in 1904, having been laid out by J.H. Taylor, an open champion, and was 'one of the finest inland courses in the kingdom'. The captain in 1910 was the current *News of the World* match play champion, Tom Ball. By 1920 a two-storey clubhouse had been built with twenty-three bedrooms and the old clubhouse had been given over to the ladies. Bramshott Halt railway station was opened 100 yards from the clubhouse. It was an 18-hole 6,020 yard course with 200 members when it closed in 1939. Harry Varden held the professional record with 73.

North Hants Golf Club, 1912. The clubhouse and grounds on the Minley Road were The Beeches, owned by Mr Bloore – an affluent London timber merchant. The remainder of the course towards Elvetham belongs to Lord Calthorpe. The 18-hole course is 6,020 yards long and before the war there were tennis courts and croquet lawns set in beautiful surroundings. The Elvetham Estates still own three-quarters of the course, and with the coming of the adjacent Railroad Heath development, rearrangement of a few holes will have to be made.

Polo match, 1926. The Wellington Polo Club's ground was attached to Ancells Farm in Cove Road and stretched up to Brook House. The grounds were close to the Minley Road and the derelict pavilion was demolished when the M3 was built. In the playing season (March to September) three meetings a week were held, plus four tournament weeks. There were three playing pitches, one being reserved for the ladies, and a practice pitch.

Indian grooms and the stables, 1926. Invariably an overseas team would be guests of the owner of Ancells Farm for at least one of the tournaments, and opponents would be invited by the Wellington Club to play the guests who would tour in this country for the season. The grooms lived in the tack rooms.

Jim Heanes. Born in Salisbury, he moved to Fleet when he married in the 1920s. Before the war he was a keen trialist and scrambler riding Ariel and Matchless machines, whose factories gave him support. After the war he opened a garage with Jack Foster, another keen motorcyclist, in Crookham village, later moving to Dogmersfield where Foster and Heanes (under new ownership) can still be seen. His hobby was restoring old motor-cycles and showing them at historic machine events at home and abroad.

Ken Heanes. Ken was fortunate to be apprenticed to Archers of Aldershot (another famous motor-cycling family). He first competed at the age of twelve, gaining a trophy in an event at Hartley Wintney, and last rode at occasional events at sixty-three – fifty years in the saddle. He rode in trials and scrambles (now moto cross), gaining over 300 awards, including the '100 mile scramble' trophy on three occasions. He became a member of the British team to ride in the Olympics of motor-cycling (ISDT) in seventeen consecutive events, gaining ten gold and three silver medals. Having ridden all over Europe and the USA, he retired from riding in 1971 and became British team manager until 1975.

Holland Birkett. After buying 3 Pondtail Road, a workshop/garage was added to enable 'Holley' to pursue his hobby of tuning and modifying his Austin 7 to get better petrol consumption in order to eke out his wartime ration. With the end of the war Austin 7s and Bugattis were stripped, rebuilt and sold on to provide funds for his passion of competing in night navigation rallies, time trials and economy runs. He is here pictured at Hindhead on a night run. 'Holley' was instrumental in founding the 750 Club, the Veteran Sports Car Club and the Hants and Berks Motor Club, all of which are still in existence. He gave a creditable performance when he competed in the Monte Carlo Rally on several occasions, and his name is still perpetuated in the 'Birkett 6 hour race' at Snetterton.

No. 3 Pondtail Road, 1943. In 1910 the building was a hand laundry and by 1929 it was a dogs' hospital. Holland Birkett took over in 1941 as the resident vet and used the old laundry as a surgery and as a home. In the early days his wife Joan partitioned the building to provide rooms for the family, which soon included two daughters. As well as helping in the surgery and looking after the kennels Joan became a very successful breeder of Pyrenean Mountain dogs. They left Pondtail in 1964 after Holley and his third wife were tragically killed in a light plane crash.

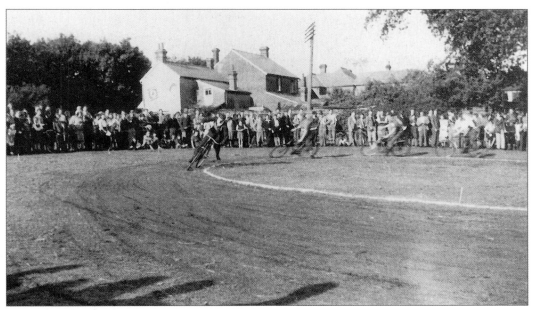

Cycle Speedway, 1949. The original track was laid out in the Firs Meadow, which is where the police station was built in 1967. Friendly matches were held on Sunday afternoons and attracted a crowd of two or three hundred. Ian Hester is leading this race, at one of the first meetings.

Cycle Speedway Track, 1952. In 1951 Fleet Council leased the club a piece of ground behind the cricket field, where the pitch and putt course is today. With the help of friends and parents the area was cleared of bushes and laid out as a 300 yard circuit with an electrically operated starting gate, cinder track and safety fencing. The inaugural meeting was screened by BBC (South) TV and the Fleet Falcons rode against the Stoughton Greyhounds. In 1954 one of the semi-finals of the British Riders Championship was held on this track. The Falcons could boast 500–600 spectators at each meeting.

Tug of War team, 1941. The Fleet Civil Defence team are competing in their first competition during War Weapons Week. The team was, back row: H. Vickery, J. Cox, W. Hook, G. Longhurst, T. Godfrey, B. Belcher, H. Silver; front row: S. Scoffield, W. Barton, -?-, and S. Culver. Transport during the war was by cycle, and the team and their supporters often appeared at Guildford, Woking and Basingstoke. After the war the club was renamed Fleet and in 1946 took part in the AAA Championships at White City; they were still pulling well in the late 1950s.

Moto Ball, 1949. The game was played by members of various motor-cycle clubs, and this was a match between Fleet and Basingstoke. The sport was very popular between the 1930s and the 1950s with the only requirement for a pitch being a fairly flat field with grass. Matches were held on several occasions on The Views in Carnival Week. Home games were played at Causeway Farm, Goddards Farm or Queen Elizabeth Barracks. Away matches were played as far off as Cheltenham, Bolton, Ipswich, Maldon and South Molton.

CHAPTER EIGHT

INDUSTRY

Pool's timber yard, 1902. Mr Herbert Pool moved from the Oatsheaf area along Fleet Road towards the northern entrance of the Hart Centre. Across the road, above the property adjacent to the old post office, can still be seen the ornamental P & S (for Pool and Son): the whole of this block was used for offices with builder's yard and joinery works behind. The old wooden Priory was the stables. Across the road were the sawmills, which in the First World War had a large contract to supply timber to the War Office. The rails on which the bed, or track, ran were discovered under the floors of the two shops demolished in 1989.

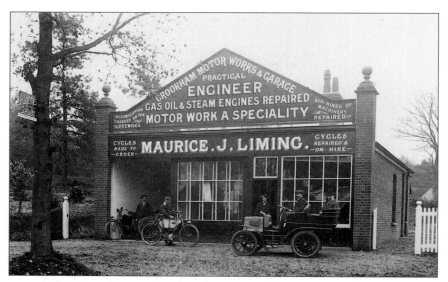

Liming's Garage, 1903. This garage in Aldershot Road was on the site of the present garage opposite The Verne. The Limings were a large well-known family who had lived in Crookham for at least 300 years and could at times boast a policeman, publican, schoolmaster, builder and sailor. The car is a 1901 or 1902 Coventry-built MMC which cost 350 guineas, and the motor-cycle in the centre is probably a Birmingham-built 2¾ h.p. Quadrant costing 42 guineas.

Atlas Motor and Cycle Works, 1920. Built in the early years of the twentieth century for Mr George Kennedy, this garage was just below the site of Gurkha Square car park and remained a garage until 1936. The side and rear walls remain but the frontage is now three shops. By 1909 it was Halimote Garage, leased to the Aldershot and District Traction Co. as motor engineers. By 1919 Mr Ridler owned the Atlas Works where he built two- and four-stroke motor-cycles and repaired cars, including the Model T shown here, no doubt. From 1919 to 1935 Stevens Bros were in residence; in the latter year the garage closed.

King and Bartlett, 1904. The premises to the left were in use in the 1820s and were the original site of worship in Fleet. In 1922 a large table top was still in the workshop: it was said to be where dissenters sat around the table to talk and read the Bible. Tom King started his coachbuilder's business here in 1905, building any type of horse-drawn carriage or 'special' as required. Mr Bartlett only remained his partner for about ten years. The business closed in the late 1920s and Mr Davies took over. The two-storey building is adjacent to the property next to St James Road in Crookham Road.

Enticknap's Garage, 1925. Mr P.J. Enticknap built his garage in Crookham Road adjacent to Coxheath Road in 1922, and being the only garage in that area business was always brisk and he stayed there for ten years until Mr Welch took over. After the war Stevens used the building as a store for several years before a block of flats was built on the corner. The make of the motor-cycle is unknown but the car on the left is a 1915 Model T Ford. On the right is another Model T, a 1925 van belonging to Mr Irvine – whose bakery was along the road opposite The Lea.

Stevens' Garage, 1930. Mr Stevens chose a prime site along Fleet Road to set his five sons up in business, and opened here in 1902 when he foresaw that the motor car was going to be big business. Two of his sons became proficient at starting and maintaining Col. Wilkes' (of Ewshot Hall) Rover car. A telephone call would have the two lads dashing off on their bikes to get the car working. Two of Col. Wilkes' sons had moved to Birmingham, designed the Rover and gave the first one to their father. Stevens were soon appointed distributors for Rovers and today their successors (now in Albert Street) still hold the franchise. Fleet's ambulance (driven by Stevens staff) was parked in the open-fronted building to the right of the showroom.

Royal Dairy milk float, c. 1930. The coachbuilding side of Stevens' business was carried out in a two-bay brick building in Albert Street. In the early 1930s Stevens produced this float to a new design: rubber tyres, three wheels for a smoother ride and the driver partially sheltered from the weather. They built hundreds before horse-drawn was replaced by electric after the war. This dairy was in the Fleet Road opposite what is now Gurkha Square car park from 1907 until the 1940s.

Horse-drawn carts, *c.* 1923. A selection of floats, traps and waggons are lined up in Albert Street outside the wheelwrights and farriers area that Stevens occupied from the Hart Centre north entrance along towards Church Road to the two grey stone panelled shops in Fleet Road. The whole block went through to Albert Street. Paint shops for cars and the wooden vehicles were all in this road. These buildings disappeared when Stevens closed in 1967, and gradually County Commercial Cars spread along Albert Street up to the roadway by the garage.

Milk floats at the station, 1935. At the Farnborough end behind the Up platform there was a 'roll on roll off' siding where Stevens' milk floats were loaded on to 'flats' for delivery. Hundreds of floats for Express and United Dairies were sent up to London from the station over the years. In the 1950s and '60s County tractors were also sent from this siding.

County six-wheeled truck, 1930. County Commercial Cars came to Fleet in 1929 when the company was formed, and used Pool's old steam engine shed at 127 Albert Street. In the early days a new Ford four-wheeled truck was converted to a longer six-wheeled model. After a few years County supplied Ford at Dagenham with springs, a centre axle and various other special parts, and the six-wheeler was built on the Ford assembly line at Dagenham. This view shows an early vehicle outside 127 Albert Street, and the shop on the left is on the corner of Upper Street. During the war every barrage balloon (land-based) was attached to one of these six-wheelers.

High clearance vehicle, 1946. After the war County set about finding a new product and they soon obtained an order for six 4 ft high clearance vehicles based on WD surplus Ford War Office Trucks No. 6 vehicles to spray blackcurrant bushes. Next came an order for two similar vehicles but with 7 ft clearance (shown here) for spraying cordon (single-stemmed) apple trees. The biggest problem in those days was obtaining materials: large diameter tubes, steel plate, large tyres and wheels, etc.

Crawler tractor, 1947. County next received an order from a pest control company for five narrow-track tractors for carrying spray equipment between apple trees and in hop gardens. Evaluation was carried out at the same time on a wider (52½ in gauge) machine and this was the resulting tractor, which continued in production until 1967. Thousands were built over the years and at one time in the mid-1950s there was an additional assembly line at Longparish near Andover: forty to forty-five were built each week. The original had a 29 h.p. engine and cost £795.

County 1884, 1982. This 188 h.p. four wheel drive was the most powerful and last tractor introduced by County Tractors (as the company was now known) before they went into receivership in 1983. Four-wheel-drive tractors had been manufactured from 1958 and were sold all over the world with hundreds of different pieces of equipment mounted on the basic machine. Drilling rigs, cranes, welding equipment, cement mixers, tipper bodies, winches, scrapers, dozers and fifth wheel couplings were just some of the accessories. 1998 was the fiftieth anniversary of the first production machines, and there was a large 'Tracks Across the Field' club event, at which many County tractors came back to Hampshire and did a weekend's work.

Marsh Laundry staff party, 1948. The staff are in their decorated canteen with the owners Mr and Mrs Marsh, possibly about to enjoy the Christmas entertainment. The laundry occupied part of Richard Pool's site from Fleet Road (a small shop) through to Albert Street along Upper Street. The business opened in 1943 and soon had a contract for many of the service units from as far as 40 miles around. By 1947 the number of service personnel had decreased and the laundry's three vans were collecting from private houses to keep the staff of eighty busy, but the laundry joined with the Royal Herts Laundry in 1949 and the Fleet site was closed.

The Art Laundry, 1935. This laundry was in Kenilworth Road on the Avondale Road corner, and was in business from 1926 until the outbreak of war. Their 1935 Silver Jubilee decorations were spectacular for a small concern, with flags and bunting and floodlighting of the building at night. During the war Huntley and Palmer, the Reading biscuit manufacturers, used the building as an outstation; local girls were enlisted to pack the biscuits for 'war work'. There was another of these outstations in Sandy Lane, Crookham. After the war Dae Health Laboratory used the premises for the packing and despatch of Valderma Cream. The premises were demolished in the 1960s and houses now stand on the site.

North Hants Tyre and Remoulding Co. Ltd,
1948. Opened in 1948 by John Pettifor, the
firm started in a small corrugated-iron
workshop in Fleet Road close to the Station
(now Links) Hotel. At the time remoulds were
seen to be good cheap tyre replacements for
the average car. The premises were soon
enlarged, as remoulds became more popular.

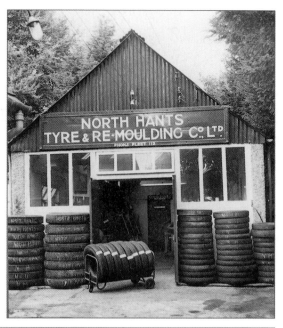

North Hants Tyre and Remoulding Co. Ltd display, mid-1950s. This display was mounted in the
marquee at the Fleet Carnival Trade Fair. Stan Burton, the Sales Manager, is in attendance.
Eventually, as remoulds became more complex as the speed of cars increased, the company became
agents for foreign tyres and wheels. The business moved along the Fleet Road to the junction of
Avondale Road.

Terrace Garage, 1933. The garage is in Fleet Road adjacent to Avondale Parade; here a new 33 C/S Matchless motor-cycle is on the forecourt. The opening to the left is today an entrance to the industrial premises behind. The building was erected for Mr Barnwell after the First World War and his motor works carried on until 1933 when Mr Langford took over. For several years the garage has been associated with the used cars next door.

Ken Heanes Ltd, 1980. In 1955 the business started in Reading Road, close to Clarence Road, in a corrugated-iron shed. By adding adjoining properties and rebuilding, a smart showroom and workshop emerged. For many years only British machines were sold but gradually Japanese and other foreign makes crept in. Ken sponsored Eddie Kidd and built the machine for his record jump over fourteen double-decker buses.

CHAPTER NINE

PUBLIC HALLS & HOUSES

Pinewood Hall, 1904. The Hall and Pearson's office block were built on the Fleet and Kings roads corner in 1903. The Hall was built as a furniture depository, although it was used in its early years as an auction room. In 1908 Mr Pearson was persuaded by some of his friends to allow the building to be used as a concert hall, as they said Weber's Theatre was a 'flea pit'. A stage was erected, and when an event was imminent the gentry's coachmen would collect chairs from the local churches and set them up in the hall, returning them the next morning. When Weber's Theatre was burnt to the ground Pinewood Hall became the public hall.

Fire at Weber's Theatre, 1914. The wooden theatre had stood for several years between Church Road and Birch Avenue in front of the present telephone exchange, and with its large stage it was a fine setting for drama evenings. It was obviously becoming dilapidated, however. The fact that it was a wooden building, together with the firemen's turn-out time, which was fifteen minutes, guaranteed that this would be the resulting picture.

New Hall, 1936. After 1918 two Army surplus corrugated-iron buildings were bought and erected side by side, with wooden panelling on the inside. Heating was by a couple of 'slow but sure' stoves, but when the audience arrived the hall soon became comfortable. The main hall had a stage and a large floor area, while the smaller hall had a good-size kitchen and serving area plus a large space that could be laid out for meals. Both floors were marked out as badminton courts. The hall was open most days for dances, plays, concerts, whist drives, etc. Fleet Mothers' Union met here monthly. The buildings on the left are the bakehouse and outbuildings of Voller's the bakers; some of the buildings are still standing.

Fleet Hall trade card, 1902. The hall was on the east side of Fleet Road 100 yards above Upper Street; the site today has one large and four smaller shops with a layby. This was a lecture and concert hall when it was opened in 1891, having been built by Pool and Son. With the coming of the early (silent) films a two-year trial began, using battery electric power and a carbon light beam to project the film. A skilled pianist accompanied the scenes with appropriate music. A Saturday matinée, with the children walking up to 5 miles from outlying villages, was very popular. The Chairman of Directors was Mr J. Oakley. The hall was demolished in 1924.

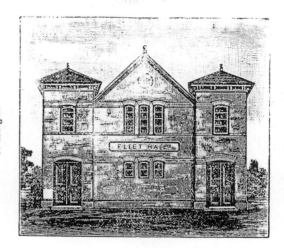

The Fleet Hall.

The above hall is carried on by the Fleet Hall Company, Limited, consisting of shareholders holding 650 fully paid-up shares of £1 each.

Directors:—Mr. J. Oakley, Chairman, Miss L. Henslow, Miss I. Foulger, W. Bloore, Esq., Rev. C. O. Munns, Messrs. Ivor Smith and J. Morgan.

Opened in 1891. Architect:—Mr. F. F. Husted. Builders:—Messrs. Pool and Sons.

FLEET HALL

Secretary: Mr. Geo. Hill, South View, Albert Street, to whom all communications respecting the hire of the hall, etc., should be addressed.

Fleet Biograph, 1921. The Biograph was the original Fleet Hall (on the right next to the chemist) and changed its name when it was converted to a full-time cinema. This was the policy of the new owner Mr Watmore, and as soon as the talkies arrived it proved a very good move.

Guard of Honour, 1928. The refurbished Biograph was reopened as The Palladium in 1928 and the Guard of Honour was no doubt recruited from a local dancing school. The following year Mr Watmore sold out to County Cinemas, which was headed by Mr C. Donado – an entrepreneur from Guildford Road. Within a year the name had been changed to King George's Cinema, and in 1936 the building was being enlarged with a restyled foyer.

Odeon Cinema, 1951. It was opened in November 1937 as the County Cinema by Florence Desmond, whose films were often shown here. By now the shop to the right had become a café, sweets and cigarette shop, and within a few years it was part of the cinema complex. At the beginning of the war the County group had sold out to the larger Odeon group who renamed the cinema. Odeon remained the last name and owner, because in 1957 it finally closed, beaten by television.

Laying the foundation stone of the Institute, Reading Room and Gymnasium in Albert Street, 1926. The building was almost opposite today's Hart Centre car park entrance, and was built before the turn of the century. It was given by Col. Horniblow, owner of The Views and one of Fleet's biggest benefactors, as a memorial to Queen Victoria. With the loss of Fleet Hall for meetings, concerts, etc. (it was by now a cinema) another hall was required, and in 1926 the Church decided to build a new larger building on the site. The foundation stone was laid in November 1926 by Edgar Figgis of Courtmoor House, seen here with the Vicar Wilson Pearce and Fred Snuggs (on the right), the builder. The stone is now in the end of Victoria Court, the block of flats eventually built on the site.

Selling bricks, 1926. The new Institute was built by public subscription and hundreds of bricks were bought by the public for 6d each. The hall was let for many functions including concerts, dances, whist drives, horticultural shows, pantomimes, gang shows, blood transfusion, mother and baby clinics, and plays. The Vicar Wilson Pearce is seen here selling bricks on the day the foundation stone was laid. With the increase in population and in the age of the hall it was a great relief when in 1973 the Assembly Halls (now the Harlington Centre) were opened, and the Institute was demolished.

Air Rifle Club, 1909/10. There were two air rifle clubs in Fleet at this time, one based at the Institute and the other at Fleet Club (now the British Legion) in Clarence Road. There was also a rifle club in Fleet with a range behind the Oatsheaf towards the cricket ground; another club at Crookham used an army range near the Wyvern. Both air rifle and full-bore rifle shooting were very popular at this time, with ranges open several times a week for matches or practice shooting.

Choir and orchestra, 1934. The annual concert given by George Hodkin and his orchestra and choir was one of the highlights of the year in the Institute. The show this year was *Merrie England*, given with pianist Miss H. Caley. The capacity audience was always appreciative of the performance. Mr G. Hodkin was headmaster of Crookham School from 1931 until 1950.

Fleet Boys' Club Annual Social, 1936. The Boys' Club Social was a grand affair with all the boys smartly dressed. The boys had use of the hall three nights a week; various games, including billiards (two tables) and table tennis, discussions and lectures were provided. Charlie Roe from the Reading Road photographers was a long-time leader.

Church pantomime, 1952. For many years the Church staged a pantomime in the Institute after Christmas. Many members appeared year after year, proving that they were willing to give the audience a good laugh at their expense. A pantomime is still part of the Church's Christmas festivities, with the show now being held in SS Philip and James' church hall.

Dr Falkland Cary. Born in County Kildare in 1897, he was educated at Trinity College Medical School, Dublin. He took a break in studies to join the Royal Navy during the First World War. On qualifying he joined a Harrogate practice, which he later headed. Here he found some time for amateur dramatics, playwriting and production. Dr Cary moved to Fleet in 1944 and soon found there was no amateur dramatic society. He soon had a card in the window of most shops and at the first meeting seventy-five people turned up, with most of them joining to form Fleet Players. The Institute, which by now was the church hall, seated over 200 and had a large stage, and for about twenty-five years all the plays (usually three a year) were performed here, before the Assembly Halls were opened. Dr Cary always found time to bring his West End and professional experience to the local players. He wrote and collaborated in more than sixty plays including *Sailor Beware*, *Watch it Sailor*, *Rock-a-bye Sailor*, *Big Bad Mouse* and *Madam Tic-Tac*. Philip Weathers and Philip King were two of his co-authors. Dr Cary also wrote novels with A.A. Thomson and a handbook on play writing. He lived in a large house close to the junction of Kings and Fleet roads. He had a very large model railway layout in a converted stable to which many guests were invited to 'run trains at Irish Railways'. Dr Cary died in April 1989.

The Queens Head, 1896. Situated on the island at the junction of Pilcot Hill, Chatter Alley and Church Lane at Dogsmerfield, it would have been built some sixty years earlier to serve the local farm labourers. Being on an island site and in a conservation area, the pub has kept much of its original charm. May's Brewery was in Basingstoke and in the brewery upheaval after the war it was bought out by Simmonds of Reading.

The Chequers Inn, 1929. Situated in the Crondall Road out of Crookham village, close to the canal, it is an eighteenth-century building which has had close associations with the canal. It was awarded the first contract for boarding canal employees and horses used for towing barges along the canal tow-path. Canal Cottage over Chequers Bridge is believed to have been the office of the original canal company that traded from 1794.

Wyvern Arms, 1928. The Wyvern was opened in the 1860s, having been built by Mr Maxwell Lefroy. A wyvern is a winged mythical creature with two legs, and is also the emblem of the Crondall Lefroy family. The building of a public house by Mr Lefroy must have raised a few eyebrows, as he was supporting Crondall and Dogsmerfield churches and he had just built churches at Crookham and Fleet.

Crookham Street Social Club, 1909. The club was built on Mr White's farmland in Crookham Street and stands 100 yards down the road from the Black Horse. Most of the cash to build the club came from local benefactors. In the 1950s, with the relaxing of the betting laws to allow gaming machines (one arm bandits), the club soon had sufficient funds to build a two-storey building on the site. The club is still thriving today.

The Fox and Hounds, 1947. Along Crookham Road backing on to the canal, this inn was built in the early years of the nineteenth century and was a welcome stop to rest and refresh the crews of the barges going up and down the 37-mile canal. In 1838 (the busiest year) the total tonnage passing on to and out of the Wey Navigation (near Weybridge) was 33,879; there is no indication of loads carried, say, from Odiham to Ash, but many barges passed each day. Fox and Hounds landlords through the years have always known how to make extra revenue from the 'back gate'.

The Oatsheaf Hotel, 1906. Crookham Common, part of the Great Heath, was traversed for hundreds of years by merchants on horseback or later in horse-drawn coaches, as Reading Road was the track from Reading to Farnham and the Crookham, Fleet and Minley roads connected the farms of Crookham to the Fleet Mill and beyond to the Hartfordbridge Flats. What better place to put a hotel in the early 1840s than on this busy crossroads? With the growth of Fleet from the 1850s the hotel prospered, but outwardly it is the same today as when it was built.

Broadway Club outing, 1933. One of Warren's coaches, parked by the old Council Offices in Albert Street (close to Upper Street) is ready for a seaside outing to Bognor or Southsea. The Broadway Club opened in the Broadway in Kings Road in about 1908, and by 1933 fine premises had been built behind two houses in Albert Street. The club is now brick built and has been extended several times. It offers fine facilities for its members.

Lismoyne Hotel, 1932. This was the year in which it opened in Church Road opposite Lismoyne Close. The hotel, approached by a winding rhododendron-lined drive, was enlarged in 1970 when a block of bedrooms was added behind the house to the left, the catering area was enlarged and the function room was built. The hotel was converted from Lismoyne, a large house built in the 1880s, one of several in the area built at the same time.

The Station Hotel, 1915. In 1880 Mr Brown of Bracknell built the hotel by the two-track Fleet Pond station, with large stables and a yard. A bowling green and a tennis court were provided. As this trade card shows Mr Wallbank was catering for a sporting clientele. The horse and motor cabs belonged, no doubt, to Mr Kimber, who used the ground along Fleet Road from Kings and Avondale roads to break and graze horses. Road widening and straightening of Minley Road up to Station Bridge meant that the hotel grounds have become very much smaller.

Station Hotel outing, c. 1932. Every year Mr Dodds the landlord (third from the right, with the bow tie) would organise a trip to Bognor or Southsea using the local coaches from Warren's of Sandy Lane. This view on the beach only shows the men, as no doubt the ladies were left at home while the men enjoyed themselves. Mr Cousins, on the left in a cap, worked for many years on the Elvetham Estate before going to Ancells Farm in 1926 when the Polo Grounds were without a groundsman. He had several men under him during the summers when the matches were played.

ACKNOWLEDGEMENTS

I would like to thank the following individuals and organisations, without whose assistance the book would not have been possible. Mr and Mrs R. Allen, G. Baker, G. Barson, Mrs E. Beale, Mrs E. Bell, Mrs V. Birkett, T. Black, W. Boulter, S. Butt, V. Carr, Mrs G. Cousins, Mrs Q. Davies, B. Dove, E. Eales, R. Eales, Mrs E. Field, A. Fitzpatrick, Hampshire Regiment Museum, Mrs D. Hannawin, K. Heanes, Mrs C. Heathers, I. Hester, P. Holmes, S. Knight, Miss J. Marsh, J. Mill, National Motor Museum, J. Pettifor, RAMC Museum, M. Rich, Mrs M. Roe, Mrs E. Ruffle, J. Rushbridge, Mr and Mrs G. Shaw, D. Small, D. Tapp, D. White.

Although there are over 200 photographs in this book I am sure that there are many more tucked into old cupboards or drawers somewhere in Fleet. If this encourages people to search out their old photographs and allow them to be reproduced there could be a second selection! It would be very sad if such items of interest were to be mistakenly consigned to the bin or a bonfire and lost forever.

Every effort has been made to establish copyright and permission has been sought to reproduce material where appropriate.

PART TWO

FLEET
A SECOND SELECTION

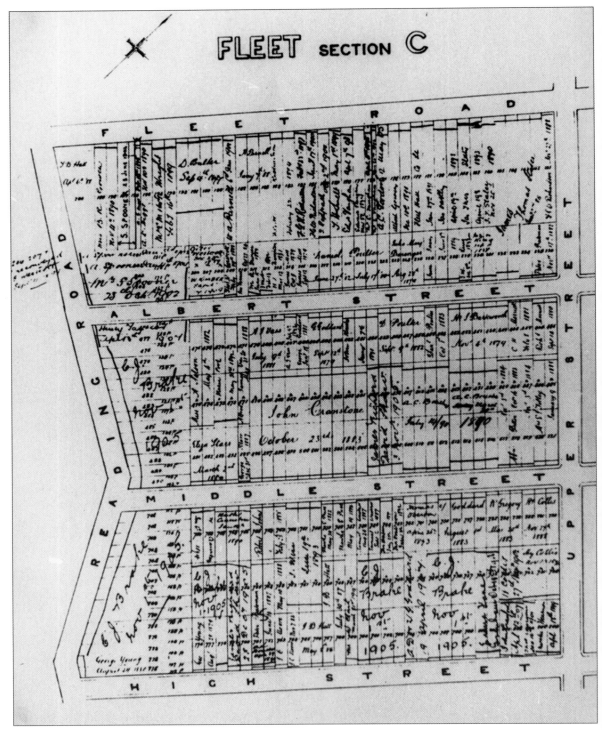

Mr Brake's map of the south-western end of the heathland he bought in 1878, showing the road layout, the plots and the names of those who had bought them.

INTRODUCTION

Fleet, originally in the Hundred of Crondall, was in the Tithing of Crookham and probably derived its name from the 130 acre pond at the north end of the town. The pond, the largest in Hampshire, was known in ancient times as Flete, and it was an important fishery in the medieval period. It became Crown property when the army came to Aldershot in 1854. The pond was designated a Nature Reserve in 1972 when it and the surrounding areas were bought by Fleet Council.

Merchants and travellers have crossed the heath that is now Fleet for hundreds of years. The Reading Road was part of the track between Farnham and Reading, while the Fleet Road connected Crookham Village to the mill and on to Hartford Bridge Flats. The siting of the Oatsheath inn at this 'busy' crossroads was no coincidence. With the coming of the London & South Western Railway to Fleet in 1847, the Station Hotel (later the Fleet Hotel and now the Links) was built and these were the only two public houses in Fleet until recently when four more sprang up at the top end of the Fleet Road.

The Whyte Lyon at Hartford Bridge (half a mile beyond Hartley Wintney) was Fleet's post office from the early 1700s until the railway came and took over the business from the stage-coaches. All letters originally had to be taken to and collected from the mail room at the coaching inn, where passengers would also join the stage-coach. Off-loading and loading was achieved in the three minutes it took to change the horses. In 1843 the London & South Western Railway Company reached Winchfield and was promptly given the franchise to carry the mails as it gave a faster and cheaper service. The main post office for the whole district was then based in a house in the station yard. Jessetts, at the lower end of Crookham Street, were appointed by the GPO to handle the local mail. By 1871 Windover and Dougherty's grocer's shop opposite the Oatsheath inn was Fleet's first post office. When Fleet Pond station (to the west of the railway bridge) was opened, the Fleet post was handled here as a sub-office of Winchfield, the mail being stamped with a 'Fleet Pond' post mark.

Fleet was granted Urban District status in 1904 and a council was elected with nine members representing the population of 2,000 and with a rate of 9*d* in the pound. With a growing population and the inclusion of Church Crookham, the number of councillors rose to fifteen in 1950. After the government reorganisation of local councils in 1974, the Hartley Wintney Rural District Council joined Fleet to form Hart District Council. Now the old Urban District area has twelve councillors.

By the end of the war in 1918 recreational pursuits in Fleet were varied, with football, rifle, golf and cricket clubs. Within a few years hockey, motor car and motor cycle clubs were started, and all attracted many members. Various hunts used Elvetham, Minley and Bramshill estates, as well as vast tracts of army ground. Fishing was permitted on the canal and pond. Tweseldown racecourse was the venue for three or four steeplechase meetings a year. Marching bands were popular and at various times you could join the Wesleyan, Drum and Fife, Salvation Army, Fleet Brass or Silver bands.

Traffic flow in Fleet was no problem in the first half of the last century except for the ten days in June when the Aldershot Tattoo was held at nearby Rushmoor Arena. Nearly half a million people came to watch the spectacle, arriving by car, charabanc and special trains. Up to forty double-decker buses were run by the Aldershot & District Traction Co. to meet each of the special trains that came from all over the country most nights. Hundreds of locals would line the Fleet and Kings Roads to see vehicles that we had only heard of. In those days Kings Road only saw the milkman, the baker, the coalman, and the regular 8A bus and about four cars daily, plus the occasional tank!

Church Crookham and Ewshot, south of the Aldershot Road, housed a few thousand soldiers in three barracks but the closure of Haig Lines in 1955, Leipzig Barracks in the 1960s and Queen Elizabeth Barracks in 2000 means that for the first time in a hundred years no troops are stationed in the area. The Gurkhas, who were loved by all the local residents, finally left for their new barracks at Sheerness in July 2000 – they had been based at Crookham from 1971.

Change in Fleet has not always been rapid and the work of the early photographers allows us to recreate a vivid history of the area beyond the immediate past. The photographers of the early postcards were rarely if ever named on the cards and it is only used cards that are dated. Many of the early cards were simply 'published' by a shop such as Radfords, Chorley, Bond and Crick, and the man behind the camera, often a local, received no credit. In the 1920s the name 'Roe' started to appear on postcards and photographs, and it could still be found on 1970s cards. They published thousands of photographs of the local area, revisiting the same places every five or six years.

Most of the photographs in this book are from the first half of the last century, while some are as recent as the 1970s. Some people may think it strange that these are 'old' but they record sights already lost to us.

CHAPTER TEN

LAND & WATER

Redfields House. Built by Mr Atty in 1879, the house occupies up to 20 acres in Redfields Lane. It has not altered much over the years and in a hundred years it has only changed hands four times. No doubt St Nicholas' School will be at the old house for many years to come.

Growing tobacco. In 1896 Mr Brandon bought or leased several fields in this area of Crookham where he grew cereals, hops and tobacco for many years. Tobacco was grown for several years on fields where the garden centre stands today. Note the original canvas-sided drying sheds. In other fields could be seen hops climbing 20 feet up their supports.

Drying tobacco leaves. By the 1930s the drying sheds had a stacking arrangement for the leaf-carrying frames to be hoisted from floor to roof. The sheds had slatted timber sides and earth floors to provide the correct conditions for drying and curing.

Harvesting the leaves. The leaves were cut and secured to drying frames to prevent bruising before being loaded on to the wagon. The average crop was 700/800lb per acre.

Bringing home the cows. Mr W. May had a dairy in Bowenhurst Road from 1910 till 1937. After milking in the morning he would take his cows along the Aldershot Road to the War Department field opposite the Wyverne where they grazed all day on the rifle range which was generally only used at weekends. Returning home on his tricycle he would then have to deliver the milk from a churn attached to his trike. In the evenings he would fetch the cows home and they stayed in the dairy until morning.

Hop picking. The whole of the area from Hartley Wintney down to Alton was planted with many acres of hops. In the late nineteenth century there were three breweries in Hartley Wintney and at least six in Farnham, plus the Crowley and Courage breweries in Alton all processing the local hops.

Whole families would turn up to help with the hop harvest. This family group was at Crookham in 1929. When the flowers were ready for picking they had to be gathered quickly as they would spoil if left in the sun or rain.

Hops were ready for harvesting in September and with Brandon's farm at Crookham, Howlings' at Cross Farm and Whites at Grove Farm – all with crops that required picking in a short period – there was always a shortage of workers. The Day Book at Crookham School on several occasions reports that 'many children were kept at home to help with the harvest'. This also applied when the corn and potatoes were gathered in.

Picking the hops started at daybreak when the dew kept the flowers large and open, and continued until about 9 a.m., by which time the atmosphere was drier and the flowers were closing up. Payment was made by volume and not by weight. The contents of the baskets were measured and then taken to the kiln. Once dried, then the hops were ready to be sold to a brewery. The kiln between Hitches Lane and the Green, now a listed building, is the last remaining example in the village.

Mr Edward Tudgey going fishing. His father Fred Tudgey opened a nursery in 1880 and later bought a piece of land in Pondtail Road and built another nursery there. This developed into a flourishing business which he sold in 1909; it subsequently moved to a larger site further along the road. He is seen here going fishing with his rods over his shoulder and equipment on his back.

The receipt page for the first year's trading of Tudgey's Nurseries. Flowers and produce were evidently being sent all over the country.

By 1909 Mr Tudgey had decided to specialise in maidenhair ferns on a large scale and he bought several fields between what is now Crookham Road and the canal, close to the Fox and Hounds inn. He erected large heated glasshouses and was soon selling ferns to customers all over the country, mainly for table decoration. Other areas were set aside for flowers and vegetables. During the war lettuces and tomatoes were grown in the glasshouses and potatoes in the fields.

Mrs E. Tudgey checking the plants in the glasshouse. After fifty years of intensive cropping the soil was poor and the glasshouses were past their economic life so the nurseries were moved to Pilcot Road in Crookham Village in 1960. Here, the fifth generation Tudgey is still in business. The Crookham Road site was developed as the Sycamore Crescent and Fern Drive housing estate.

Ice-hockey team. A team of local lads in the 1920s ready to take on all comers. Even if their sticks were a disadvantage for ice-hockey, at least they could limp home with their support.

Ice-hockey, 1920. The pond froze over every year and annual ice-hockey tournaments were held here, with some teams coming from the London area. From 1847 special trains were arranged at weekends and evenings to bring skaters from London to the pond. From 1847 to 1869 the stop at Fleet was called Fleet Pond station.

Feeding the swans. When the pond froze over volunteers went out every day to ensure that no wildlife was trapped in the ice. They would break the ice so that the birds could drink and also provided food for the water birds.

Fleet Pond, often called the Lake. Up to the 1930s, it boasted a fine sandy beach at its eastern end which attracted dozens of families for picnics and swimming. No doubt the effect of draining the pond during the war allowed scrub to grow on the 'beach' and now only a small area of sand remains. The staging stretching out across the water is all that remains of the Royal Aircraft Factory's platform for launching early float-planes.

Fleet Pond and the surrounding area have been designated a 'Site of Special Scientific Interest' and over a thousand species of plants and animals have been identified in the 133 acres. The Pond Society and Hart District Council work together to maintain and improve the nature reserve.

Swimming pool and Fleet Pond. This was the view from the Up platform of Fleet station, looking towards Cove Road, from the 1930s to the 1960s. On the left is the swimming pool. Built behind a large new house in the mid-1930s, it remained open for thirty years. Houses now stand on this ground. In 1971, when the M3 was being built nearby, the owners of the whole of this view allowed contractors to dump thousands of tons of soil and gravel in the pond by the Cove Road before the Council noticed the illegal act. The night club/restaurant now stands on this site.

Gathering rushes. Poulters Bridge Cottage in the 1930s was a smallholding with various animals and a couple of fields. With the canal owner's blessing, the smallholder used to cut the rushes by the canal bank close to Poulters Bridge and his family would transport them home ready to thatch the hayricks.

When the canal burst its banks at Crookham in 1961 the canal bed drained for a long way on either side of the breach. Local youngsters often spent their spare time at the swing bridge opening and closing it for boats to pass, knowing that the boat-owners would tip them at least sixpence. After the breach the lads seized the opportunity to look in the mud for the coins that had fallen short – apparently several pounds worth were found and were shared among the boys.

The Howard family, 1916. The landlords of the Fox and Hounds inn close to the cemetery could always make a little extra by catering for the people using the canal at the back of the premises. Between 1916 and 1936 Mr and Mrs Howard ran a small fleet of boats for hire by the hour. Mr Howard's family is seen here in a couple of boats at the Fox and Hounds in 1916. Today's landlord organises a successful boat festival every year.

Canal regatta. For several years a carnival day on the canal has been part of Fleet Carnival Week. The earliest events were held soon after the canal had been dredged and restored. This is the 1992 event with the decorated boats pictured at Reading Road Wharf ready to set off to the Fox and Hounds. The return trip was made after dark with all the boats imaginatively illuminated.

CHAPTER ELEVEN

TRANSPORT

Many of the local gentry had a horse-drawn vehicle in the early years of the twentieth century. Often the coachman would take the master to the station and then be available to take the lady wherever she was going. Here we see Mrs Waitham Long who lived in Adcote in 1905, almost opposite today's Vicarage in Branksomewood Road. The coachman is Mr Ian Moore, who lived in Victoria Road.

Bert Watts, milkman. The Watts brothers moved to Great (or Lower) Bramshot Farm before 1910 and built up a first-class dairy herd. Tom and Dick ran the farm while Bert delivered milk and dairy products around Fleet and Crookham with his trade bike. Two churns were secured in the front carrier and a third hung from the handlebars – he would have needed to make several trips a day back to the farm. The fourth brother, James, set up another milk-round with a horse-drawn float based in the Station (now Links) Hotel yard. Tom and Dick sold up in the mid-1920s but the two milk-rounds carried on through the war.

Mrs Emma Grit, chimney sweep. In the first half of the twentieth century most houses were heated by open fires burning coal, wood or peat, with chimneys taking the smoke up above roof level. The soot (a very fine oily powder) which stuck to the inside had to be swept out regularly to prevent fires. A 12-inch ring of hard bristles formed the brush head, which screwed into 5-foot-long flexible wooden rods and was pushed up and down the chimney, dislodging the soot, until the brush appeared out of the top of the chimney pot. This must have been very dirty and unhygienic employment. There were always eight to ten sweeps in the area but at sixpence per fireplace the rewards were good and steady. Mrs Emma Grit of Clarence Road was the only lady sweep recorded in Fleet and she is seen here chatting to Mr Harden outside his butcher's shop in the Fleet Road. Both started their businesses in the first few years of the twentieth century but Mrs Grit seems to have 'retired' after the First World War.

Lindfield's decorated van. Lindfield's ladies' and gents' outfitters were located by Lloyds Bank in the Fleet Road from 1936 to 1940. They decorated their 1937 9hp Singer Bantam van for the varied events in coronation year. They also boasted the 'Finest lending library' in town.

Vincent's decorated car. Vincent's the butchers had premises in Kings Road at the junction with Clarence Road. They decorated their car to show off their products at the various events between 1935 and 1939, such as royal celebrations and carnivals. Mr Vincent built the house, with shop attached, in 1906 and the family business survived until 1982.

Motor mower at the polo grounds. When the polo grounds first opened in 1925 the mower was pulled by horses but within a few years a motorised version appeared. An old Citroën car was stripped of its body and bonnet, its rear wheels were replaced by spiked metal wheels about 9 inches wide and a steel plate was fixed over the engine to keep the rain off. The blacksmith from Stevens' Garage in Fleet Road carried out the conversion. The vehicle was capable of pulling a triple set of mowers giving a cut 15 feet wide. It lasted until the club closed in 1939.

Golf club tractor. This was a Ford Model 'N' modified by Pattersons for working on golf courses. Pneumatic front tyres, wide steel rear wheels with short spikes for grip and a tipping body were the main features. The special sand in the bunkers had to be changed every year and topped up on a weekly basis. There were at least fifty bunkers on the course so the tractor was rarely idle, as the sand was stored by the car park of the North Hants Club in the 1930s.

Cane's delivery van. In the 1890s Mr Cane came to Fleet and bought Windover & Dougherty's small wooden lock-up shop and post office on the Oatsheaf corner. He employed three men to solicit orders from the 'big' houses and errand boys to quickly deliver the groceries and soon built up a noted business. By 1913 two delivery vehicles had replaced the errand boys to give a better service. This 15.6hp Wolseley CA van was one of the first grocery delivery vehicles in Fleet.

This 1926 11.9hp Morris Cowley 'Bullnose' was no doubt one of the first cars bought by Bradley Mathews and they obviously used it locally for publicity purposes. The advertisement proclaims '73 hour non-stop engine trial. Get our list of 30 other bargain used cars.' Their garage was modern in appearance, with an attractive office frontage. The two pumps and showrooms were in Fleet Road, almost opposite Stockton Avenue, with workshops behind going through to Albert Street. A paint spray shop was built, which in the 1950s was occupied by a DIY business. The garage closed at the onset of the Second World War.

Aldershot & District bus. The Aldershot & District Traction Co. was founded in 1906 with only one or two routes and it was not until Christmas 1912 that there was a service to Fleet. This service via Crookham cross-roads eventually became the No. 8 route and terminated at Fleet station, where this 40hp Daimler CC is shown. The conductress Elsie Ridgers must have been one of the first 'clippies' employed, and her family worked on the 'Traco' for many years. The company bought eight of these buses in 1913/14, five of which received new larger bodies in 1920/22: they were obviously very reliable.

Dennis charabanc. This may be one of Mr Lukey's later vehicles which regularly took club and public house outings to the coast, usually Bognor Regis or Southsea, in the 1930s. With the arrival of pneumatic tyres, passengers had a quicker and more comfortable ride.

Coach outing, 1930. In 1927 Mr Warren of Atbara Road bought a fleet of ten Guy buses and operated the Fleet Coaching Co. as well as running a Fleet to Aldershot bus service. Most of his vehicles were engaged in private hire. Here he is in 1930 picking up a club, possibly at the New Hall for a seaside outing.

A Red Cross outing. Fleet Coaches are seen here picking up the members for an outing organised by the Fleet Branch of the Red Cross. Regular trips were run by the Fleet Branch for many years for the elderly and infirm. Jack Rushbridge was the driver on this day.

Sunday School outing. For two or three years before the outbreak of war in 1939 the Methodist Sunday School Superintendent Charlie Perrin organised an annual outing to Bournemouth and Swanage by special train. The various Sunday Schools in Fleet would pay for the children to have a day out at the seaside – for many it was the only time they saw the sea. The train would be ten to twelve coaches long and could carry 800 or more. Any surplus seats would be offered to other children and their mums at a nominal fare. The train would leave about nine o'clock with its special headboard 'Fleet Sunday Schools'. On arrival at Swanage Mr Perrin would take all the children on to the beach and they would wait while he hoisted a banner that could be seen from all along the beach. At lunchtime he rang a large bell which was the signal for the children to come and get their sandwiches, cake and a cold drink. After the war the trips were revived and they continued well into the 1950s.

The Down platform, Fleet station. Fleet station was completed in 1904 when the tracks were increased from two to four. Passenger care was very important: a length of both platforms was covered to the edge and the footbridge was also covered. In the early 1920s W.H. Smith opened a bookstall adjacent to the access to the Down platform but it was forced to close in the late 1930s, probably because of staffing problems. These buildings were demolished in 1965 and a modern station – with no thought for customer comfort – was built on the same platforms.

Station Approach, Fleet, 1930s. The covered entrance where you could alight in the dry from your carriage or car can be seen just in front of the two taxis. The parcel shed is behind the waiting car and there are goods trucks on the right. The buffers stood where today you enter the car park road, just inside the station approach; there were also two or three tracks running up to the end of the car park by the pond.

Station Approach, Fleet, mid-1960s. By this time, just before electrification, the tracks in the goods yard were not used and nor was the parcels shed (on the far right). Parking areas were already being laid out – in the late 1950s and 1960s the number of commuters using the station increased rapidly, and most of them would drive to the station. Prior to the end of goods traffic no cars could be left at the station.

Wharf Cottage. An eighteenth-century cottage along the Crondall Road, just over Chequers Bridge, is believed to be the original canal wharfinger's office and home. Mark Hicks lived here from the 1920s until his death in 1966 at the age of ninety-two. Just across the canal by the bridge is Crookham Wharf, where all the coal, bricks, timber and so on which was carried by barge to and from Crookham was handled.

When the Crookham Brick & Tile Co. ceased trading at the turn of the twentieth century not all of their barges were immediately disposed of. No. 4, a wide boat, stayed here on the canal between Poulters Bridge and Chequers Bridge for several years waiting for a buyer.

Fremlin's van. In the 1920s this brewery van came to rest against the wall of the end house of Coronation Cottages on the Clarence Road and Upper Street junction. Over the years there have been hundreds of accidents, many of them serious, on the various crossroads in Fleet. We should perhaps blame Mr Brake, who laid out the road system in 1878 'in the American style', but I suppose he couldn't foresee the mass use of vehicles fitted with combustion engines.

Tank accident. After the war many soldiers were taught to drive tanks on the common around Church Crookham while they were stationed at Haig Lines. In 1947 REME at Arborfield kept their tanks at Martins Lines close to the North Horns (now Tweseldown). While learning to drive a 1947 Sherman tank with gun and turret removed on the road in 1953 one soldier got his controls wrong in Beacon Hill Road: accelerating over the pavement and across a garden, the tank embedded itself in Laurel Cottage. It took more than a week to shore up the house before the tank could be pulled out by a Scammel recovery vehicle. Before 1956 the house had been demolished.

In 1925 W. Davies & Son opened a garage in the premises that had previously been used by Thomas King bodybuilders for several years in the Fleet (now Crookham) Road between the two entrances to St James Road. There were two petrol pumps at the back of the pavement and cars used to park at the kerbside to fill up. On one occasion in about 1947 something went wrong and the car burst into flames when the engine started – luckily nobody was injured.

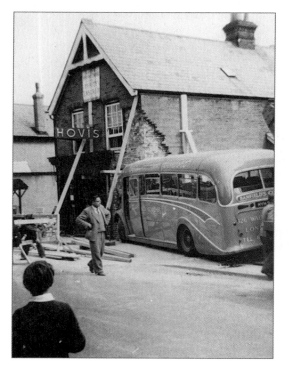

For several years a London coach used to bring air stewardesses from Heathrow to their homes in this area after their tour of duty, and collect others who were just starting their tour. On this occasion, as he was going along Fleet Road towards the station, the driver was taken ill and the coach veered across the road and came to rest embedded in the side of the shop. It was more than a week before the shop was shored up and the coach could be removed. Nobody else was hurt.

CHAPTER TWELVE

AT PLAY

Crookham mummers. The mummers seem to be peculiar to north Hampshire. The performance involves six or seven men, some playing more than one part, telling a traditional story (some say it has been the same since Norman times) each Boxing Day. Three performances are given, with a collection for charity. Trim Tram, Bold Roamer, King George, the Turkish Knight Bold Slasher, Father Christmas and the Doctor are some of the principal roles, and their costumes are decorated with strips of coloured paper. Bramshill House had a troupe of mummers and in the 1930s they used to perform on Christmas Eve.

Fleet Silver Band. In the late 1920s Fleet could boast two bands – one silver, the other brass – and there was great rivalry between the two. A local businessman who was in the Brass Band provided a piece of ground where a hut was built for the band to practise in, but with the band's demise during the war the hall was used by a Slate Club and also the St John Ambulance Brigade. The band was resurrected after the war but finally laid down the baton in 1956. The St John Ambulance Brigade eventually bought the site and built their new headquarters there in 1982. By 1929 Mr Mill, the leader of the Silver Band, had his workshop in Upper Street and he allowed the band to practise in the workshop in the evenings. The Silver Band had become defunct in the 1960s, just before Mr Mill retired and moved away.

The Salvation Army Band. This band toured the town on Sunday mornings, singing hymns and saying a few words here and there, and hoping to pick up a few converts. They went down to Crookham Village every four to six weeks and would hold a service on the green outside Jessett's shop. On this occasion, in the early years of the 1900s, they were persuaded to pose outside the shop, possibly by George Jessett who was a keen photographer.

Red Diamond Band. Regular features of the New Halls' programme were whist drives and bridge, plus meetings of women's and men's groups. The floors of both halls were marked out for badminton courts and both modern and old-time dancing always attracted a good crowd, including many soldiers stationed locally. Most of the bands were local but a ball would attract a nationally known band. Groups like the local Red Diamonds shown here in 1923 consisted mainly of young people. The drummer here was Reg Karn, who lived in Fleet all his life.

School concert. In the 1930s Crookham School had several enthusiastic art and drama teachers and their annual show was always well received, according to a couple of parents (now great-grandparents) who are still living locally.

This was the school orchestra in 1937. They were coached by Mr Dodge, a senior master. All the children would have brought their own instruments. No doubt the orchestra played at assembly on special occasions and at shows at which the parents were present.

Army Cadet Force Band, *c.* 1942. During the war the Army Cadet Force and the Air Training Corps were formed and many boys joined the local units. The training given helped the boys when they were called up into the services. After the war National Servicemen were given six weeks' basic training but those with ACF/ATC training joined at week three, only four weeks before joining their units. Company Commander Captain Hodkin and 2nd Lieutenant Salter were the two leaders until the mid-1950s.

The Scout Association, comprising older scouts, formed a band to play in the carnival each year through the 1950s and early 1960s. Dennis Mallinson was the drum major and each year the band entertained the crowd with their music and antics.

Fleet Carnival Band, 1959. Alex Fitzpatrick is leading the band. The Suez crisis had ended just before the carnival, so the theme for this year was 'The 13th Suez Canal Lancers'. Themes in other years included 'St Trinian's All Girl Band' and 'The East Cheam Colonials', inspired by the film and the Tony Hancock character respectively. For several years they borrowed their instruments from the defunct Brass Band but the band's trustees sold off the instruments in 1966 and that finished the Carnival Band.

Country dancing. Before the war, when a large proportion of the world map was 'pink', all the schools celebrated Empire Day (24 May). In the 1960s political changes resulted in the day being renamed 'Commonwealth Day'. It was the only day when the whole school assembled, together with the governors and managers, and various tableaux were performed for the visitors. In 1925 three boys and three girls gave a country dancing display. Some of these children's families still live in the Fleet area today.

Another school play in the 1930s was *Don Quixote*. Many hours would have been spent making costumes and rehearsing before the show was fit to show to the parents. The cast seem very proud of their efforts at Crookham.

Girl Guides' pageant. The Crookham Girl Guides held a garden party at Mrs Wynne's house in Aldershot Road each year to raise funds and to show how much the girls had learnt. The afternoon ended with a pageant, which this year was entitled 'Cries of London'.

Dancing around the maypole, 1925. The maypole was set up at in the playground at Fleet School on several occasions for Empire Day celebrations.

Cinema staff. Fourteen staff ran the cinema in 1946/7. Mr Fricker was the manager and there were projectionists, usherettes and maintenance men; they also staffed the café next door. The programme was changed (generally) on Sundays, Mondays and Thursdays. The cinema was on the east side of Fleet Road, 100 yards up the road from Upper Street. The site today has one large and four smaller shops, with a layby. A lecture and concert hall was opened on this site in 1891 and it showed early silent films and soon became a full-time cinema. In its long history it had been rebuilt once and also enlarged, but it closed in 1957.

Fleet Players. This production of *Journey's End*, set in the trenches in the First World War, was produced in the spring of 1954 at the Institute in Albert Street. Dr Falkland Cary, a prolific playwright who wrote and collaborated in more than sixty plays, founded the Players soon after he came to Fleet in 1944.

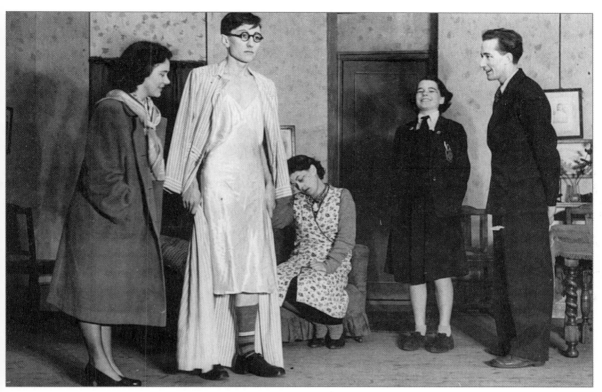

Fleet Players in a scene from the spring 1950 production *Bed of Roses* by Falkland Cary. The stage at the Institute was of a good size and the hall seated more than 200. From 1945 till 1971 all productions were staged here.

Fleet Players in *Night Must Fall* by Emlyn Williams, which was produced in November 1952. With the opening of the Assembly Hall (now the Harlington Centre) in 1972, all future productions were held in the modern hall. There were a few problems initially with the acoustics but they were later overcome.

Fleet Players won publicity by appearing in the Fleet Road on the Saturday before the show in their costumes, and selling tickets on the spot. These were advertising *The Bride and the Bachelor* in October 1959. Dr Falkland Cary died in 1989 and ten years later the curtain finally came down on the Fleet Players.

The Beverley Hillbillies. One entry in the 1964 Carnival processions featured the Clampits, a very popular American television comedy. Characters included Granny, Jed, Jethro and Ellie May. They were portrayed by the staff of Edna's, the ladies' hairdressers close to the old post office in the Fleet Road. The car looks rather grand and is obviously rare as it could not be identified by the National Motor Museum!

This is Mr Bowers' delivery van decorated for a carnival procession in the early 1950s. The Bowers family ran a grocery business for several years in Fleet Road from premises close to the old cinema site.

Firemen's float. For several years in the 1950s and 1960s Freddy Manfield and a couple of his firemen mates would hitch a trailer behind his car and with a bucket of water and a ladder would keep the carnival crowd amused and on their toes. Somehow they also managed to fill several collecting-boxes on the way!

Fleet Carnival Band. Some of the bandsmen used their own instruments but most borrowed them from the now defunct Brass Band. As well as taking part in the main procession, they would also parade with the children on the Saturday.

This is County Commercial Cars' entry in the carnival procession, with their own tractor towing the two trailers. The first had a drive mechanism which turned the carousel and made the horses go up and down; the second trailer carried the band and clowns. Between the 1950s and 1960s Stevens Garage, Technograph & Telegraph, and County Commercial each entered a tableau. They were always of a very high standard and by 1965, when Technograph moved to Bracknell, the honours of being the cup winners was about even in the commercial tableau class.

'Tulips from Amsterdam' was another carnival entry by County Commercial Cars, again with two trailers being towed by one of their tractors. The windmill blades were turned by the trailer wheels, and the scene was set off by a Dutch band and dancers. For several years these floats were also taken to Basingstoke Carnival but this stopped when the police started enforcing the Road Traffic Act.

'Ah Men' was the Reading Road Young Wives' entry in the 1962 carnival. There was always great rivalry between the various ladies groups, most of which in those days could boast about a hundred members each.

The 'MUM' Majorettes was the Fleet Mothers' Union entry in the 1973 carnival. The procession went along Albany Road and down Kings Road in those days, rather than taking today's route straight along Connaught Road.

Robin Hood was the All Saints' Wives' Group entry in the 1987 Children's Carnival and is shown here having just turned into Fleet Road from Kings Road. For many years the first Saturday of carnival week was children's day, with all the events in the afternoon being for them.

CHAPTER THIRTEEN

RELIGION

All Saints' Church. Mr Lefroy, the squire of Crondall (which included Fleet), laid the foundation stone in 1860 in memory of his wife Janet. The church was completed by Janet's father, as Mr Lefroy died a year before it was consecrated in 1862. The marble tomb with the recumbent figures of Mr and Mrs Lefroy now stands at the back of the church.

The Chester miracle cycle. This medieval religious drama was performed at Lobswood in Wood Lane in May 1954. This scene is part of the 'Last Judgement'. The drama was in two parts, performed on two evenings, and there were three complete performances spread over six days. Originally written by a monk of Chester Abbey in 1228, the plays were revived at Chester during the Festival of Britain in 1951 and repeated the following year. This production was only the third since the reign of Elizabeth I and was performed in medieval costume.

The trade card of Mr Parsons, wood and stone carver. Mr Parsons lived in Elms Road from the end of the First World War until the 1950s. In the 1920s he built a new house next door to his home – at this time there were eleven houses on this side of the road and only one on the other (Kings Road) side. Over the years he helped Mardles the stonemasons, especially in 1920 and 1921 when they were busy making the war memorials for Fleet, Elvetham, Ash, Crondall, Crookham and Hartley Wintney.

The first vicar of All Saints' was the Revd William Henry Plummer who was appointed in 1861 and served Fleet until his retirement in 1895. He was the longest-serving of the Fleet vicars.

Mrs Harriett Plummer, wife of the first vicar. Mr Plummer spent only a year in retirement, dying on 8 August 1896. His wife continued to live in Fleet until her death on 23 July 1908, aged ninety. They are both buried in the churchyard close to the chancel wall.

Fleet Roman Catholic Church. In the early 1900s services were held in a private house in Fleet, and the first church was built in 1908 on the corner of Connaught Road and Kings Road. By 1934 it had been enlarged, and again after the war, and by then it could seat 172. This building is now used as meeting-rooms and a hall. Pictured is the 326-seat church which was built by the side of the existing church in 1965.

Interior of SS Philip and James' Church, 1936. Built in 1900, construction was simple and cheap, with corrugated iron sheets fixed to the wooden frame, and wood panels on the inside. It was known as the 'Iron Church' or 'Tin Tabernacle'. After the Second World War there was obviously a need for a new church closer to Pondtail where the population was greatly increasing. Lobswood in Wood Lane was bought by the PCC in 1951 and it was here that the Chester miracle cycle was staged. Fernhurst in Kings Road was bought in 1957 and it was decided to sell Lobswood. The new church was built in Kings Road in 1966.

The Revd Pughe used to invite the parishioners to come to tea parties on his lawn on fine days. He was vicar from 1913 to 1916. In 1932 the vicarage in Branksomewood Road was bought and the Church Road site was sold. Renamed Glebe House, it was demolished in the 1960s and Glebe Court was built on the site.

All Saints' choir. This group includes Mr Pope the organist, Mr Prideaux the Albert Street School headmaster and Mr Edwards his deputy. Mr S.C. Mardles and two of his sons are also pictured on All Saints Day in 1901. Girls were not admitted to the choir until the 1950s.

Methodist Sunday School. Built in about 1908, the main building in Branksomewood Road behind the church had a stage at one end and could seat a hundred people. On the left was a smaller room with several sinks and ovens and plenty of tables; this room was hired by the Albert Street School for domestic science classes and every Monday morning the girls from the top two classes marched from the school for their lessons here as there were no facilities at the Fleet School.

The Revd J. Stuthard Mercer was the minister between 1922 and 1933, succeeding the minister appointed in 1914 when the Congregational church was built. In 1964 a Sunday School hall was built by the church and in 1999 planning permission was granted for radical alterations to be made to it.
The Presbyterian Church of England and the Congregational Church united to become the United Reformed Church in 1972.

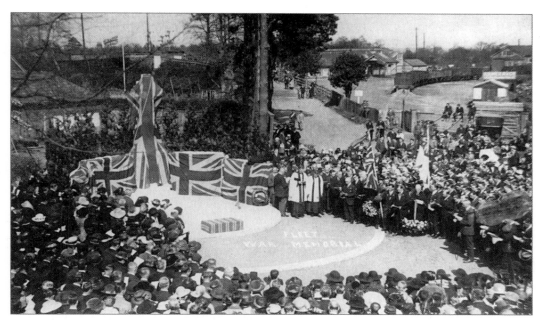

When the Cenotaph in Whitehall was unveiled in 1920 many towns decided to build their own memorial and Fleet was no exception. A site backing on to the Station (now Links) Hotel's bowling green was chosen and Mardles the local stonemasons were entrusted with the job. On 10 April 1921 the Earl of Selborne, MP for Fleet, unveiled the memorial, and the clergy of all the churches read prayers and the dedication.

Fleet war memorial. This photograph was taken on a normal working day soon after the unveiling: note the absence of traffic. The coal trucks can be seen in Station Approach, where cars are parked today. The memorial was moved to a site close to the library in the 1970s owing to the increased traffic flow and resulting noise during the Armistice Day service. It was moved to its present site in the car park when the new civic offices were built in 1986.

Christ Church, Crookham, was consecrated in 1841 by Bishop Sumner of Winchester for the parish of Crookham-cum-Ewshot and could seat four hundred. When the Guildford Diocese was created in 1927 Christ Church left the Winchester Diocese.

The interior of Christ Church. As happened in the 1840s and 1850s in some other churches in the south the congregation segregated itself here. The women sat on the south side and the men on the north, the girls near the harmonium by the vestry door and the boys beyond the pulpit.

Crookham Church. In 1841, when the church was dedicated, Anthony Lefroy was the first curate. In 1875 the Revd Gordon Wickham was appointed curate and when he left in 1883 his brother Wilfrid took his place as vicar, a position he held until 1925. In 1971 a meeting room and new vestry were added. The original building is connected to the extension by the south porch.

Crookham war memorial. Subscriptions poured in for this and a simple cross on a stone base was ordered from Mardles the Fleet stonemasons. It was erected close to the church at the junction of Gables Road and was dedicated on 10 October 1920. After the Second World War the base was altered to include the fallen of that war.

Elvetham Church. St Mary's stands in the grounds of Elvetham Hall but was closed for services in 1969. The church had been rebuilt in the Norman style in 1840 at a cost of £4,000, with traditional Hampshire flint facings. There had been a church on this site since 1250.

Elvetham war memorial. This memorial by the church close to Elvetham Hall was mainly paid for with estate money. The church became derelict many years ago and no Remembrance Day ceremony is held here. The memorial was unveiled by the Hon. Sir S. Arthur Gough-Calthorpe who was the Commander-in-Chief, Portsmouth, and the dedication was performed by the Bishop of Winchester. A thousand people attended the dedication ceremony on 22 April 1922. The names of fifteen village men lost in the First World War are inscribed on the base.

Chapter Fourteen

Industry & Health

Lismoyne Hotel in Church Road, opposite Lismoyne Close. The hotel was converted from a large house called Lismoyne which was built in the 1880s. It was one of several in the area built at the same time. The hotel opened in 1932. Extensions were carried out in 1970 when the catering area was enlarged and the function room and a block of bedrooms were added. Further alterations to the catering area were carried out a few years ago.

Bob Karn shoeing a horse in his blacksmith's shop in Connaught Road in 1909. Two of his sons, Joe and Reg, are with him. His house was called Jubilee Cottage but within a couple of years it was renamed The Forge. He lived here until 1935, but with the change of owner it had reverted to Jubilee Cottage within twelve months. When he first had the forge there were only three houses on the south side between Aldershot Road and Upper Street.

An early trade card for King & Barlett, a partnership that lasted about ten years. Tom King started the business in 1905 and with his partner he offered a very wide range of crafts. King & Bartlett and Stevens Brothers were among the first car repairers in Fleet. Their premises were in Fleet (now Crookham) Road, between the two entrances to St James Road.

Davies & Sons' garage. The company was founded by William Davies and his son, another William, and opened in these premises in 1935 in the Fleet (now Crookham) Road between the two entrances to St James Road. In 1947 the firm's first coach was bought. This picture shows the premises decorated for the coronation in 1937. The garage business closed in 1957.

The pumps and showrooms. The large showrooms were built opposite the original premises in the 1950s, and additional garages were built to house several coaches.

The paint shop, Stevens & Sons. In the 1930s the painters and signwriters here would have been kept busy painting the boards for farm and diary vehicles, as well as repairing cars perhaps after an accident, or in a new colour at the owner's whim. In the words of their brochure: 'A special feature of our work is our painting, lettering, etc., as we realise a high class finish proves a good advertisement for our clients and ourselves.'

The body building shop. Stevens & Sons, carpenters, were kept busy building dairy and farm vehicles, including hundreds for London's Express and United Dairies in the first half of the twentieth century. After the war a large batch of ex-army International lorries was reconditioned in the workshops to be used by British hauliers, as new vehicles were almost impossible to obtain. Then they started to build mobile library vehicles and there were always one or two in the workshop. These brought the Library Service to villages and outlying areas.

Stevens' Brothers' Garage. By the early 1950s the petrol pumps had been moved here, to what had been an empty piece of ground. During the war the site had housed a static water supply tank – about 6 feet high and 30 feet in diameter – which would enable fires to be put out even if the mains water supply had been cut. There was also a smoke room on the site. Stevens' Garage ran from the north entrance to the Hart Centre along the Fleet Road towards Church Road, and the whole site stretched through to Albert Street behind.

Rolls-Royce station wagon. In the late 1940s Stevens Brothers converted this pre-war car into a 'commercial vehicle' so that it would qualify for unrationed 'red' petrol – private cars could only use the 'white' rationed petrol. Several luxury vehicles were converted as there was no indication of when rationing would end. Here are some of the staff (left to right): Messrs Shorter, Chittenden, James, Legg, Skeates, White and Baldock, all long-serving workers.

County Commercial Cars' workshop. Founded at 127 Albert Street, here they had their workshop and drawing-office; across the road at no. 122 a couple of small offices were rented. In 1936, when Fleet Council vacated Ruby Cottage (no. 121), County moved their offices so they were all under the same roof but by 1955 they had bought the back of Claremont (nos 84/96) along the road and built new workshops and offices here. They gradually occupied the former Stevens' buildings (as pictured here) in the late 1960s. The white building on the right is the present car showroom and garage, but all the other buildings have made way for the Hart Centre and the car park entrance.

Tractors ready for shipment. By now the trading name was County Tractors and the despatch area was here at the Station Trading Estate. Generally, the 'cabbed' tractors were for the home market while those within (in the foreground) were for export. Note the heap of shale on the left: this was the residue from power stations which was used by the factory next door, Hemelite, to make breeze blocks for the building industry. They operated here from the 1950s to the 1980s, when they were taken over by Tarmac.

County Tractors always tried to supply a machine to meet the customer's needs and this was the result of one unusual enquiry. The customer wished to carry out seismic soundings for gas and oil exploration in the North Sea off the Dutch coast. Another order was received for machines to farm small islands off Tasmania. County took the opportunity to use the Sea Horse for publicity purposes and in July 1963 David Tapp crossed the English Channel in it from Cap Gris Nez to Kingsdown near Dover – and immediately set to work harrowing a field! The tractor floated at sea, and was propelled by the deep lugs on the soft-ground tyres as the wheels turned.

Technograph & Telegraph. This company's premises were on the corner of Albert Street and Upper Street and included the old Pool's furniture depository and yard, together with the Marsh Laundry site. T&T came to Fleet in 1954 and stayed until 1965 when they moved to larger premises in Bracknell. When the premises were vacated County Tractors moved in, and they stayed until 1983. Eventually the site was cleared to make way for the Hart Centre.

The print and inspection shop at T&T, pictured in the early days before the two-storey extension was built in Albert Street. The girls on the right are inspecting the finished products while the men are operating printing presses. The main product in the early days was a strain gauge, made by the etched foil process. It was made from a special resistant metal which reacted differently when subjected to strain either in compression or in tension modes.

The press shop at T&T. This is where the circuit board parts required to make the components were cut, punched and shaped. The company was originally called Techno Electronic Products and was started in a small production unit in the East End of London, where Dr Paul Fisler (who invented the etched foil techniques) evaluated the practical uses of their products. Eighty people worked at Fleet in 1965 before the company moved to Bracknell.

Huntley & Palmer, the biscuit-makers from Reading, had to increase production at the beginning of the war and this was achieved by turning over the whole factory to production with packaging being carried out by dozens of small workshops around Reading. There were two such places in this area. One was in Kenilworth Road on the corner with Avondale Road, where the Art Laundry stood before the war. Dae Health Laboratories moved in here in the late 1940s. The other place was in Sandy Lane in the building that formerly housed Warrens' buses. Here all the staff are enjoying themselves at their Christmas Party in the Institute in 1954 or 1955. As young men were called up for the services during the war, young women were 'called up' for essential domestic work to free up enough men.

Dae Health laboratories. Sited on the corner of Avondale Road and Kenilworth Road, the premises were built in the 1930s for the Art Laundry and after wartime service with Huntley & Palmer the Dae Health laboratories took over the front building. When they closed in the early 1960s houses were built on the site. Biscuits were still packed in the rear building until about 1956.

Albert Social Club. The club was founded in 1906 and made its home in the Albert Hall (later used by the British Legion) in Clarence Road, but in 1922, after internal problems, a new clubhouse was built on Mr Blacknell's paddock in Albert Street. Arthur Lunn was the first steward and served for many years. The club has had several extensions, the most ambitious being the two-storey function room and steward's flat added in 1963. The membership had reached eight hundred at one time. The club is still open.

The Broadway Club was founded before 1910 in first-floor premises at 4 The Broadway in Kings Road and moved to their present home in Albert Street, in premises behind 115 Albert Street that had been a builder's yard between 1930 and 1936. The building had a corrugated iron exterior with wood panels inside. By 1969 the changes in the gaming laws had allowed sufficient money to be raised to build a larger brick building for the four hundred members. In the last forty-five years there have been only two stewards, Harold Cox (a lifelong Fleet resident) and now Chris Powell.

A Hospital Sunday gathering on the green in Crookham Village, at the junction of Crookham Street, Crondall Road and Pilcot Road, 1909. This was the venue for most of the village events. Here the Salvation Army Band are playing for the hymns and the ornate banners are paraded – doubtless most of the village turned up to join in.

The Nurses Home was built in the early years of the twentieth century for nurses from London hospitals to convalesce after illness. While at the Home the nurses wore blue cloaks with matching bonnets. Eventually the Home moved to the south coast and the building, next to the Congregational (United Reform) Church, was sold. The house has now been demolished and an elderly residents' complex stands on the site.

Fleet Hospital was erected in 1897 after public subscriptions had raised £444; Lord Calthorpe gave the ground and £888. Over the years public subscriptions have raised the money to provide gas, electricity and the sewerage system. The eight-bed hospital increased in size and in 1948 it was taken over by the NHS. Over the last twenty years outpatient facilities have been added and its future seems secure.

Thurlston House. Situated at the top of Victoria Road, this very large house set in large grounds, was built in the 1890s. During the First World War the house was used as a Red Cross hospital for soldiers wounded in France, and some two dozen local women, domestics and VAD nurses tended the injured. After the war the house was returned to private ownership. The last owner was Col. Anson McCleverty who lived here from before the Second World War until 1960, when the building was tragically burnt down as the result of a workman supposedly setting fire to the roof. The council later bought the site and built houses and a block of flats for elderly people.

CHAPTER FIFTEEN

GROUPS & PARTIES

Fleet School opened in 1886. The block shown here fronted on to Albert Street. It was to accommodate 130 children. By 1910 the block fronting on to Church Road was built as the infants' school. The playground was fenced to ensure the boys did not mix with the girls or infants. The toilets were at the bottom of the playgrounds. When the church wanted to build this school, Mr Brake, who had bought most of the heathland that is now Fleet, sold eighteen plots (each 40 feet wide) at half cost. In 1947 the senior children moved to Heatherside School and in 1960 the juniors also transferred to Heatherside when the seniors had moved on to the new Courtmoor School. This photograph shows the infants celebrating the centenary of the Albert Street School. Not long afterwards the infants' school moved to the newly built Velmead School.

Fleet School, Standard 3, photographed in 1926 in the playground. There was a narrow concrete path against the wall of the infant school in this area but the main area was cindered.

Fleet School, Standard 3, 1931. These boys were ten years old. School photographs like these were very popular in the 1920s and 1930s, and it is not very often you see examples outside this period.

Fleet School, Standard 5. This photograph was taken in 1929, with the class posed in the girls' playground against the dividing railings. The fir trees close to the fence gave lovely shade on hot summer days.

Fleet School. These are the ten- and eleven-year-old pupils in 1947. Mr Fletcher (right) was the 'big' school's headmaster (his wife was headmistress of the infants' school) and he is pictured here with Mr Butler and his class. With forty-five pupils in the class, the imminent move to Heatherside School was certainly necessary. The move came in September that year and it allowed the juniors who were left to occupy all of the Albert Street block, with Henry Taylor as headmaster. It was only two or three years before the Fleet and Heatherside Schools were overcrowded because of the postwar population explosion. The corrugated building on the right is the canteen, which was built on the boys' playground and was often used as an emergency classroom.

Fleet School celebrated Empire Day with the Scouts and Guides wearing their uniforms and bearing the 'flags of all nations'. Here we see a 1930s parade getting ready to march around to the playground. The school governors would be present and the chairman would present the prizes to the top girl and boy and give a short speech. The children would then be given the rest of the day off. This was the only day when parents were welcome at the school.

Fleet School, Standard 6. Another class of forty-plus pupils, pictured in 1929 in the girls' playground. The surface was loose cinders – very hard on hands and knees if you fell on it.

Fleet School, Standard 3, 1932. This photograph was also taken in the girls' playground with the outbuildings, including the cycle sheds and coke store, shown in the background. The coke fuelled the one 'slow but sure' stove in each classroom. At this time the classrooms were illuminated by two gas lamps hanging from the high ceiling.

Fleet School, Class 3, photographed in 1931 against the wall of their school in Church Road. These were the five-year-olds in their first year at school. For many years they were under the care of Miss Hawker.

A class at Crookham School pictured at their two-seater desks in the 1920s. Two children sat side by side at each desk, with individual hinged lids allowing access to their books and pencils inside. Fleet School had similar desks. At the back towards the right can be seen the chimney pipe from the 'slow but sure' coke fire which supplied the only heat in the room.

Crookham School. This is the top class of the junior school in 1959, pictured in the playground. These children would have gone on to Courtmoor School or a grammar school in the following September.

The 1st Crookham Girl Guides. This group photograph was taken in Mrs Wynne's garden in Crookham's Aldershot Road in about 1950. In those days they met in this area but today Fleet and Crookham guides share the Basingbourne Road headquarters.

The 1st Crookham Girl Guides on parade in the early 1940s on the clear sandy area between the Aldershot Road and Tweseldown racecourse. There was nowhere else for them to parade at that end of Aldershot Road.

The 1st Crookham Girl Guides parading along Aldershot Road past the saluting base in 1942 during the Crookham Warship Week parade. In previous years a War Weapons Week and a Spitfire Week had been held to raise extra money to help the war effort.

The Crookham Scouts approaching the saluting dais on the steps of the cinema in Fleet Road during the 1940 Spitfire Week parade. The idea of the various 'weeks' during the war was to encourage every body to buy 15 shilling Savings Certificates, thereby providing money which the government could use to buy planes and weapons. There would be a daily ceremony during the week when the 'indicator' (sited by the clock tower) would be adjusted to show the total collected.

Members of the Women's Land Army. During the Second World War young men had to register for the services when they reached their eighteenth birthday, so young girls were drafted into essential work at home. The Women's Land Army was the largest non-military group, with many volunteering to work in nurseries and farms. Tudgey's nurseries and the farms at Crookham and Crondall all had their share of WLA girls.

The Westover Road Victory party in 1945 was held in the Institute in Albert Street. Most people in Fleet, especially the children, enjoyed a party in their street with everyone contributing tables and chairs and making sandwiches and cakes in spite of the tight rationing. After five years of war everybody worked together.

Victory party, 1945. The Elms Road area was only sparsely populated in 1945 but the thirty houses brought out many children and teenagers to sit down to what must have been the best party most of them could remember.

On Coronation Day, 3 June 1953, many groups and streets organised tea parties after the main celebrations in London had finished. This party in Westover Road saw bunting hung up around the garden and tables laden with party food. The coronation brought a tremendous surge in sales of television sets and this was the first time people could see a coronation without moving from their armchairs, even if it was only in black and white.

CHAPTER SIXTEEN

RETAIL

*Mr E. Hayes opened his shop in Fleet Road adjacent to Stevens' Garage in 1925 and
stayed until 1935 when he moved into Reading Road South, six shops along from
Tower House on the Oatsheaf crossroads. The shop is now run by the third generation
of the family and is a specialist shoeshop and shoe repairers. In the 1920s the
business advertised as 'Boot Maker – Repairs a Speciality' and 'Tobacconist'.*

Walter John Edwards was born in 1870 and started working for Sydney Parsons, the butcher at Odiham, in 1896 doing a milk-round. Two years later he was sent to Hook station to collect his boss's brother Albert, who had just returned from Australia. They immediately became firm friends and in 1898 Albert opened his butcher's shop in the Fleet Road close to Church Road, with Walter working in the slaughterhouse behind the shop. At the onset of the Second World War the slaughterhouse became redundant but Walter worked in the shop until he retired in 1948. He moved to Connaught Road in 1925 and stayed there until his death in 1960. A lifelong Methodist, he joined the Royal Berkshire Regiment in 1915 and served in France where he was wounded and gassed.

Irving's Store. These premises, backing on to the canal at the top of The Lea, were built just after the First World War and comprised a house, shop and bakery. Mr Irving, pictured here with his Model 'T' Ford van, continued his business until just before the Second World War. The bakery business finally closed in the mid-1950s and the 'corner' shop suffered the same fate as most other corner shops, closing in the 1960s.

C. & E. Roe Ltd. This business was started by Mrs Florence Roe who lived in Aldershot Road in 1924 and continued by her husband Charles who built premises in Reading Road in 1927 opposite Albert Street. In 1962 he built a colour laboratory to the right of the shop. This was the only place for miles around capable of processing coloured prints and trade was good for several years until other premises were allowed to install this equipment. The car outside the shop is Mr Davies' American Studebaker, a very rare sight in Fleet in 1947.

The staff of C. & E. Roe, 1932. In the early 1930s quite a few staff were employed to run the shop and the print-processing. Included in this photograph are Charles Roe and his son and partner Edward (Ted), who wrote the book *Mainly about Fleet and Crookham*.

Woodman's Store, 4 September 1939. All the placards are declaring Hitler's defiance to our demands. John and Olga Woodman opened their grocery shop here in 1932. The premises had been built in 1896 as a double-fronted shop for Mr Raynor's hardware store. He also sold paraffin. Mr Wise later opened his pastrycook and confectionery business in the left-hand shop, but in 1946 both parts were under Woodman's name.

Woodman's Store. By 1950, with more and more houses being built in the Pondtail area, including Velmead Road, more floor-space was needed at the shop and a single-storey extension was added where an off-licence was opened. John and Olga Woodman retired in 1981 and today a butcher's shop and a supermarket occupy the site. The building has been a shop for 104 years.

Pondtail post office in Kings Road opposite Wood Lane. Owned by Mr Fowlie, it opened in 1905, when there were five collections daily from the wall post-box outside. Mr Fowlie was the sub-postmaster until 1936. This early picture shows the two outside gas-lamps which illuminated the window and the forecourt. This was a grocer's and greengrocer's nearly a hundred years ago and it is still a 'corner' shop serving a wide area and selling the same range of goods together with the post office facility.

Vincent's shop. On the corner of Kings Road and Clarence Road, this butcher's shop was built by Harold Vincent in 1906, together with living accommodation and stabling for a horse. He also bought an acre of ground in Pondtail Road where he raised chickens to provide eggs and fresh meat for the shop. The business continued to thrive in the hands of his two sons Leslie and Derek but it eventually closed in 1982.

Nelson and Goodrick opened their draper's store in 1903, selling a very wide range of goods with courtesy. If an item was not in stock, it would be quickly ordered. There were branches in Aldershot, Farnham and Farnborough, each managed by a member of the families. The business closed after the war owing to shortages in supplies; customers had only limited clothing coupons because of wartime rationing. In the 1960s the site was redeveloped as a modern three-storey office block, with shops on the ground floor, opposite Gurkha Square car park.

Fleet Market Place. When Oakley's (at the clock tower) was built this was the focal point of Fleet and the south side of the road to Reading Road was named Market Place, but the name did not catch on and by 1920 it had been forgotten and was never again mentioned in an address. Some properties had been built with balconies over the pavement, but nobody complained as the support posts on the edge of the pavement could be used to tether horses. Eventually the council had these extensions over the pavement removed. The building on the right is the Baptist church, in the days before it lost the 'front garden' to road widening.

A. & F. Bowers' shop. Between 1946 and 1961 the Bowers brothers had a grocer's shop in the Fleet Road nearly opposite Gurkha Square car park. On the right was a right of way to the slaughterhouse behind Harden's shop. On the left of Bowers' was a baker's with bakehouse behind. These premises have been a bakery since the First World War.

E.C. Boyes' small butcher's shop was one of several that sprang up at the end of the nineteenth century. This shop in Reading Road South stood near the Annes Way shops and only lasted a couple of years. At this period many farmers sent a horse and van to nearby towns to catch the local trade. Deliveries would be made to large houses and the meat that remained would be sold off cheaply to the locals. One Odiham farmer used to park at the Oatsheaf every day to sell his meat until he was banned.

F.G. Lanham's newsagent and tobacconist's shop in Fleet Road between the grey panelled shops and Church Road. There was a newsagent's on this site from the late 1880s until the mid-1990s. Beside Lanham's is Parson's the butcher's, and between Parson's and the corner stood Williams & Wright seedsmen and coal merchants. Their coal pens were to the side and back of the shop until 1960.

This was Cane's shop on the northern corner of the Oatsheaf crossroads until the family sold the shop in late 1950s. Within a short time it reopened as Holland & Barrett's groceries but with the major road-widening scheme at the crossroads in the mid-1960s the shop and the Baptist church next door were demolished and replaced by today's parade of shops with offices over.

Richard Pool's office on the right stood next to what is today the NatWest Bank. Richard Pool was a haulage contractor and furniture remover, and was the earliest horse-bus operator in the area. His business was founded in the late 1800s and survived within a few hundred yards of his office until the 1950s when it was taken over by Cantay's of Basingstoke. By the 1920s these houses with front gardens were gradually built along to Victoria Road, and then one by one a shop was built on to the front. Since the 1970s most of these have been demolished and rebuilt with a wider pavement.

W.H. Smith. This newspaper distributor had a franchise to have a newspaper stall at Southern Railway stations and space was provided at Fleet on the Down platform for a kiosk in 1926. After the war the platform offices were reorganised when British Rail took over and there was no room for the kiosk so a separate shop was built against the station railings. The station was rebuilt in 1966 when the track was electrified, but the shop was not rebuilt.

Grove Stores. Built about the time of the First World War, these premises in Reading Road South, close to Annes Way, are still trading today. Between 1933 and 1939 William Corderoy ran a general grocer's shop here, while next door Mr Clark had opened his hairdressing business in 'The Shop'. He stayed there until about 1970, and the shop is still a hairdresser's. In the 1950s the house to the left of the shop was called Silver Park and for several years Mr William Lunn ran a nightclub here. The site is now Silver Park Close, stretching back to Corringway. Several small shops were opened up along this stretch of the Reading Road but have since disappeared.

Acacia Café in Beacon Hill Road, late 1940s. Byrne's grocer's and newsagent's stood next door to the café on the corner of Aldershot Road. At the time the Molay family owned the café and Crossways garage was on the opposite corner. Note the WD stone with its broad arrow on the back edge of the pavement by the side of the shop: this indicates the military boundary. These stones were placed along the boundaries of the land that the army bought in the 1860s. Today many such stones can be seen around the pond and along the canal near Pondtail Bridge. The ground around the camps at Crookham were also marked.

CHAPTER SEVENTEEN

SPORT

The Stevens brothers entered the annual London to Brighton race several times with their 1904 De Dion. It is seen here in the 1930s at Marine Parade with Redvers Stevens driving and Syd Farr navigating. When it was not away at a show, this car was kept in a prominent place in the showroom at the garage.

After the war car and motor cycle events were very popular and they often took place on the vast tracts of army ground around Aldershot. One very popular sport was car rallying. Holland Birkett, the local vet and rally specialist, organised events for local touring car clubs which would cover the ground from the end of Pondtail Road to the tank test hills and beyond to Caesars Camp. Pictured here are Bill Davies and Jack Welch in a 10/15hp car trying to pass through an observed section without incurring penalty points.

In the early 1920s the Fleet Motor Cycle Club held meetings, navigation events and reliability runs, sometimes at night, with their small and less reliable engines. They are seen here outside the Oatsheaf, their usual meeting place, and to judge by their dress this is a social event.

Daniel Welch. With his father John at the top of his class at car racing it was no wonder that young Daniel showed interest and later an aptitude to follow in his footsteps. In 1997, driving a TONY Cart, he won the JICA class top formula for 13–16-year-olds. This season (2000) he is being sponsored in the Formula Vauxhall single-seater championship, and success could mean he turns professional next year.

John Welch in action. John's father was also successful competitively in both motor cycling and car events so it was no surprise that John was soon gaining national honours in his field. He is seen here at Brands Hatch leading Jonathan Palmer in 1988, on the track where he won the 1986 Grand Prix. During his career he was a factory driver for both Ford and Vauxhall and between 1969 and 1993 he was five times overall British rallycross champion.

Jack Welch. Except for the war years when there was no motor sport, Jack would undoubtedly have gone much further in scrambling (now called MotoCross) and as a trials bike rider. He is seen here competing in a trial on army land at Aldershot in the 1950s.

Within a couple of years after the end of the war scrambles were being organised on the army ground around Aldershot and here at Elvetham on Forestry Commission land every Sunday of the season. Races were usually over five or six laps and were for experts or novices on 250cc, 350cc or 500cc machines. This area is now called Elvetham Heath and within a few years it will all be built on. There was always a large following to watch the thrilling races, especially as there were usually several local riders.

Fleet Cricket Club. The club ground is in Reading Road North, about three hundred yards down the hill from the Oatsheaf Hotel. The ground was provided by Lord Calthorpe of Elvetham and opened in 1905. By 1910 two Saturday teams and a Wednesday team were playing regularly. Wednesday was half-day closing for the shops in Fleet before the war, so the Wednesday team comprised mainly shopworkers and proprietors. All matches were friendlies in those days. It was not until after the war that Sunday matches were played. This picture shows the players during a cricket week in the 1930s.

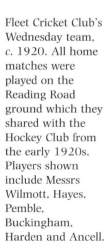

Fleet Cricket Club's Wednesday team, c. 1920. All home matches were played on the Reading Road ground which they shared with the Hockey Club from the early 1920s. Players shown include Messrs Wilmott, Hayes, Pemble, Buckingham, Harden and Ancell.

Ladies' Cricket Club. Mr Barnett farmed at Cross Farm in Crookham Street opposite Jessetts from 1928 till 1936, during which time he laid out a cricket pitch and his daughter soon established a ladies' cricket team. An empty barn was utilised as a changing room and for refreshments. Not all the matches were serious and here a team in fancy dress are having a good time. Matches were played regularly against teams from Farnham, Sherfield and Reading, and it was not long before a men's team was playing here as well. The ladies' team was known as the Barn Owls.

Fleet cricket team posing by the pavilion, 1920s. In a few years time the club will celebrate its centenary on the Reading Road ground. Previously, from about 1880, they had played in the grounds of Mr Bloore's house, The Beeches in Minley Road (now the North Hants Golf Club).

Crookham Rifle Club was founded in the first few years of the twentieth century on land opposite the Wyvern, by the (then) fire station. The ranges of 50, 100 and 200 yards disappeared during the Second World War, but the club reformed after the war using the ranges at Leipzig Barracks at Ewshot Camp. This shield was won by the club in 1920, when they used to hold regular club meetings.

Mr L.R. (Bob) Fenwick was a member of no. 5 platoon of the local Home Guard throughout the war and his experiences on the rifle range led him to join the City Rifle Club. In 1955 he won the most prestigious Queen's Prize at Bisley. A total of 1,254 competitors entered the three-day event. After firing 81 shots at distances between 200 and 1,000 yards, Bob scored 286 out of a possible 300 points, winning by one point. The Duke of Gloucester presented the prizes and Bob was ceremonially chaired by his friends and club members.

Fleet Football Club was founded in the late nineteenth century and in the early days they played at the bottom of the Views where Campbells Close is today, and later at Watsons field in Fleet Road by Birch Avenue. Lord Calthorpe gave them their present ground in Crookham Road and this photograph shows the team selected for the first match on their new ground on 3 March 1923.

Crookham Ramblers Football Club. C. Chillery, P. Savage, S. Coutts, M. Munday, F. Dudley, E. Townsend, K. Gardner, L. Galaher, P. Upwood, C. Stephens, R. Byrne, D. Oakes and mascot Les Galaher's son were in the squad for the 1959/60 season. The club was active between the 1950s and 1970s. Originally they played in Crookham Village behind the Social Club in a field lent by Mr White, but in later years they played on the Abercorn ground opposite the Wyvern inn.

Fleet Football Club. E. Wheatcroft, J. Brooks, D. Alner, R. Sawyer, J. Cook, R. Byrne, B. Gilbert, coach S. Brown, B. Stephens, J. Davidson, A. Piper and R. Silvester made up the team that played at Hartley Wintney in the 1956/7 season. Before 1961 the club played in various grades of the Aldershot and Basingstoke leagues.

Fleet Football Club. A. Wells (physio), D. Cram, J. Maitre, D. Wells, P. Paul, D. Alner, A. Bayliss, J. Brooks (Manager), B. Stephens, T. Nash, B. Arnold, L. Hardaway and J. Charlton made up the team for the first home match in Division 3 of the Hampshire League. Fleet won the league with 50 points (2 for a win) from 30 games, scoring more goals (113) than any other team in the three divisions.

Fleet School football team, 1929/30. Mr Salter coached and managed the school teams for many years. Facilities for sport at the school were very poor with only tarmac and cinder playgrounds. Pupils marched from the school to the Views in Victoria Road once a week for about an hour and a quarter and there was usually only time for a game of rounders, cricket or football – if it wasn't wet!

Fleet Football Club. R. Cox, A. Dance, M. Threlkeld, R. Thorner, P. Moss, S. Burton, R. Silvester, R. Driver, J. Godwin and D. Marley made up this minor league squad in about 1947. About this time Fleet Spurs Club was formed. They played at Oakley's Park, providing the chance for more players to play on Saturdays, but there were still only the two grounds in Fleet.

Fleet Hockey Club. Founded in 1925, they rented part of the cricket ground for their season (October to March) and from their earliest days there were ladies' and men's teams. Seventy-five years later the arrangements are just the same! This is a ladies' team ready for a home match in 1929.

Fleet School netball team. On games afternoons (once a week) the two top classes would walk from the Albert Street school to the Views Meadow to enable the girls to play rounders or netball in the top field while the boys played cricket or football in the lower field (if it wasn't wet). On Saturday mornings the girls' and boys' teams that were playing in the Aldershot and Farnborough leagues would have to travel several miles to matches. This is the 1933 netball team with their teacher.

Ladies' tug-of-war at a summer fête in about 1919. The venue is not known but the ladies' intentions seem very clear, despite what the Revd Henry Robins might say! In later years the fête was held in the grounds of the vicarage (Glebe House) and later in the grounds of the adjoining new vicarage.

Fleet War Weapons Week in 1941 was the first occasion that the Fleet Civil Defence tug-of-war team competed – in their overalls. By the following year, when the Warship Week sports day in the 'council field' came around, the 'Civil Defence' team, with more training, new jerseys and shorts, proved superior even to the RAMC team.

Tug-of-war club team with their trophy after winning the Victory Sports in the Views. By this time the war was over and the Civil Defence team was being disbanded, becoming Fleet instead, and in the next year they entered the AAA Championships at the White City. The club was still competing well into the 1950s.

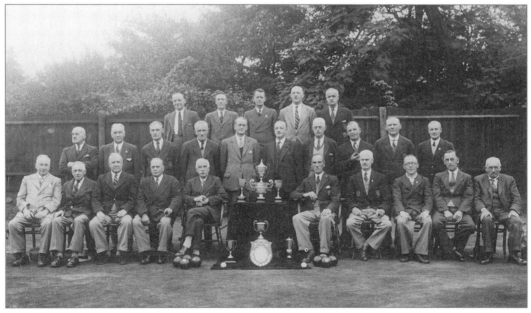

Members of Fleet Social Bowling Club pictured in 1942 with a fine array of cups and a shield. The club was founded in 1914 in premises behind the Fleet Social Club in Clarence Road. The Social and Bowling Clubs are both still very active today. There is also Fleet United Bowling Club, situated by the police station in Crookham Road – this opened in 1923 and is still thriving today.

The Fleet Cycle Speedway team pictured in 1954 before setting off for an away match. They rode against teams from a wide area and travelled in comfort in one of Davies' coaches (later known as Fleet Coaches).

Fleet Cycle Speedway track. This picture was taken during the inaugural match in 1952, which was televised by BBC South, when Stoughton Greyhounds were entertained by the Falcons. The ground, a disused hard tennis court, was rented from the council and the riders (and their parents!) cleaned up the ground and built the track, including the banking for the spectators.

CHAPTER EIGHTEEN

IN UNIFORM

The army incinerator was built soon after Aldershot Camp was established in 1855. The incinerator, with its 60-foot-tall chimney, stood not far from Norris Bridge, where the NGTE was later built. There was a constant stream of horse-drawn wagons full of rubbish from Aldershot Camp up to the start of the twentieth century when rubbish began to be disposed of elsewhere, and the chimney was subsequently leased to the RAE who mounted wind and temperature instruments on the top. When the RAE had no further use for it it was demolished in 1930. This photograph was taken by Mr Roe of Fleet, and shows Movietone News filming the demolition from the roof of a van.

Lord Roberts Camp Home. This building provided relaxation in the evenings for soldiers stationed in Tweseldown Camp (later Haig Lines) in the First World War. Constructed of corrugated asbestos and interior wood panels, it was built close to and almost parallel to Tweseldown Road but in the early 1930s it closed for a time while it was converted into a cinema showing silent films. By the mid-1930s it was 'now 100% all talking'. It was an army cinema but was open to the public, and it closed in the 1950s.

The Church Army Room, Crookham, was also opened in the First World War and provided recreation rooms for soldiers in the Haig Lines. It included rooms where dominoes, cards and darts could be played and there were also reading and writing rooms.

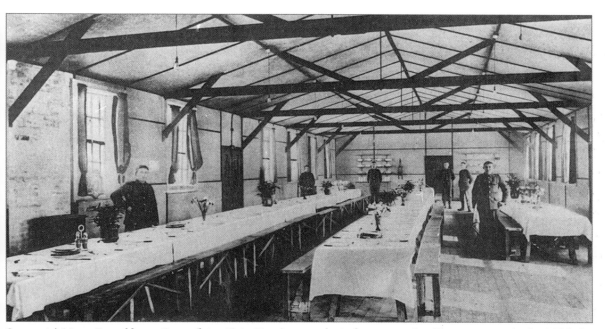

Sergeants' Mess. Tweseldown Camp (later Haig Lines) was a hutted camp at Crookham crossroads. In 1915 the RAMC moved in and the camp became their depot, and remained so until 1932 when they moved to Keogh Barracks at Mychett. The sergeants' mess was different to the men's mess, in that it had tablecloths, curtains and mess staff.

Queen Elizabeth Barracks. Formerly Boyce Barracks, this camp was built in 1937 for the RASC for basic Militia training in Sandy Lane close to the Wyvern. At the outbreak of the war the RAMC was brought back from Mychett, which was now too small to train the thousands of medics necessary and it was only in 1966 that they moved back to Keogh Barracks. In 1948 Queen Elizabeth (the Queen Mother) as Colonel-in-Chief came to Crookham on the occasion of the Corps Golden Jubilee and in her honour the camp was renamed Queen Elizabeth Barracks. The Gurkhas came to the barracks in 1971 but have recently moved to Kent, leaving the last wooden hutted camp in the country to the developers.

Territorial Army. 'E' Company, 4th Battalion Hampshire Regiment, comprised sections from Yateley, Farnborough, Aldershot, Odiham and Fleet. Company headquarters were at Redan Hill in Aldershot and this photograph was taken at Aldershot.

Territorial Army. This is the Fleet section of 'C' Company, 4th Battalion Hampshire Regiment, in 1916/18. They met in the gymnasium behind the Institute in Albert Street (now Richmond Court flats). Meetings were held twice a week and some time was spent at Aldershot. The Terriers were formed in 1908 and the men were partially trained before entering the army.

No. 1 Platoon, 'C' Company, Home Guard, of the 25th Battalion of the Hampshire Regiment, covered Fleet and Crookham. No. 1 Platoon usually met at the British Legion Hall where there was a large hall upstairs. Training took up at least one evening and Sunday each week, and more if there was any enemy air activity that week. When the siren sounded to warn of approaching enemy aircraft, everyone would parade to positions at strategic locations – at one stage in the war they were on duty every night for several months. Many nights were spent guarding the railway line and other important features from enemy parachutists and incendiary bombs.

No. 3 Platoon, Home Guard, was comprised mainly of Crookham men. They met at Dogmersfield House. As soon as the siren sounded they would be deployed in small groups watching out for enemy parachutists. No. 2 Platoon was entrusted with the spigot mortar while No. 5 Platoon had a Smith gun, which was towed behind Mr E. Tapp's car, painted khaki for the duration of the war. No ammunition was ever supplied for this weapon but 'Dad's Army' fired onions from their Smith Gun.

Home Guard officers and NCO's. No. 3 Platoon did most of their training in the 1,700 acres of the Dogmersfield estate which included woodland as well as grassland. During the war there was a defence line running across the area with obstructions along the canal between Winchfield and Crookham and across the fields to Pale Lane, where the River Hart was dug out wide and deep and defences built up to protect the nearby railway line, making it difficult to cross.

A Sunday morning route march for No. 3 Platoon, Home Guard. Initially this was no joke for a fifty-plus man who sat at a desk all week, only to find that on a Sunday morning he was expected to march 5 miles in heavy boots, wearing a thick rough uniform and carrying a heavy rifle on his shoulder. Younger people who today laugh at 'Dad's Army' are not aware that during the war a lot of what happened really was just as funny – unless it was you who fell in the muddy ditch early on a frosty evening.

In 1941 there was a Civil Defence parade and inspection on the barrack square at Crookham, when all sections of the ARP (Air Raid Precautions) were assembled in their 'action clothes' with their support vehicles. Here a section of the decontamination squad (gas dispersal) parades in front of Mr Crumplin's lorry, which had been commandeered for ARP use. On the door of the lorry the address still says Rose Farm but 'Fleet' has been painted out – it was the same on shop fronts. In addition, direction signs at road junctions and street names were all removed and if you were in a strange town you would have no idea where you were – but more importantly nor would the enemy if they managed to invade.

This is the First Aid section of the Civil Defence Rescue Squad at the same parade. They had a large fleet of heavier support vehicles. They were based at Pools, close to the station. The Auxiliary Fire Service was attached to the National Fire Service. Not all their vehicles were fire engines but they all towed a water-pump.

Fleet fire brigade. In 1920 Fleet Urban District Council replaced the pony and trap and cycling firemen with this Model 'T' Ford which would carry the equipment and the men to a fire much more quickly. In 1934 a Dennis fire engine was bought and this was the vehicle the crew took into the war and the National Fire Service.

Fleet's first fire brigade was formed in 1900 and they have had various vehicles, from the pony and trap (for hoses, etc.) and bicycles to today's sophisticated powerful engine and pump. During this time Fleet had had only four stations. This picture from the mid-1950s shows Messrs Harrison, Manfield, Ellis, Wright, Tarrant, Smith, Baker, Sub-officer Shorter, Burgess and Woolley.

Building the bonfire. For many years after the war until the mid-1960s Mr Harden allowed his field at the Firs Meadow to be used by the Fleet firemen to have a bonfire party with a giant bonfire and the best firework display for miles around in aid of firemen's charities. The rubbish for the bonfire was collected by many helpers over several weekends and the size of the finished pile can be judged by the picture. Firs Meadow was large and ideal for the many fun days including fairs, carnivals and gymkhanas held there. Mr Harden sold the Firs Meadow to Hampshire County Council in 1966 and the police station now stands on the site.

Church Crookham held a carnival during the 1930s, and here the fire engine is leading the other floats along Sandy Lane back to Crookham House, next to the church, where the procession had assembled. Crookham had its own fire engine from the early years of the twentieth century until after the Second World War but now Fleet station covers the Crookham area.

Blackbushe Airport. Hartford Bridge Flats was a 4 mile expanse of flat scrubland on either side of the A30 between Blackwater and Hartford Bridge – or at least it was until 1941 when the Air Ministry found it and decided to build an RAF airfield on the high plateau. The standard 1940 three-runway airfield was adopted with the main runway running almost parallel to the A30 and the other two crossing the A30 at an angle. RAF Hartfordbridge was actually established with the A30 still running through the middle! Soon, to avoid confusion, the name was changed to RAF Blackbushe, after the farm that backed on to the Forestry Commission land which hid the stock of bombs.

Handley Page Hermes IV. In 1946 the military aircraft moved out of Blackbushe and the late 1940s saw the arrival of Britavia, Airwork and Silver City air lines operating charter flights with Lancastrians, DC3s and Bristol Freighters. Here is a Britavia Hermes IV. Below its nose are the Silver City/Britavia radio and instruments workshops, while the distant buildings under its tail are Airwork's hangars. In the 1950s its official designation was 'London Airport, Blackbushe'. By 1955 there were 36,000 aircraft movements each year but with the opening of Gatwick the passenger business left Blackbushe and in 1960 it closed. Today Blackbushe is home to the Car Auctions who own the whole site, as well as a Sunday Market and a private flying club.

Douglas Boston IIIA. During the war many nationalities flew from Blackbushe, including Free French, Dutch, Canadians and Americans, as well as the RAF. This Boston is from 342 Lorraine Squadron which had evidently completed seven operations, as there are seven bombs painted on the fuselage. One of the four 500lb bombs carries a painted message which includes the word 'Hitler' – it all helped morale. The bombs arrived mainly at Fleet station and they were usually taken up to Blackbushe on 'Queen Mary' trailers at weekends – manoeuvring round the hairpin bend out of the station yard to get over the bridge took a lot of skill.

Spitfire engine. During Spitfire Week in Fleet in 1940, there were displays in various shops in the Fleet Road. The gas and electric showroom on the corner with Birch Avenue set up window displays pertaining to the RAF to encourage the public. At the other end of the Fleet Road, close to today's police station, Mr Davies also put on a display in his showroom. It includes two aircraft engines, one from a Spitfire, as well as various other pieces of aircraft.

Towing the spigot mortar. This weapon was obviously designed to be used by the services who could pick it up and put it in the back of a lorry, but as the Home Guard only had a car the weapon was unusable. No. 1 Platoon overcame the problem by designing and fitting a carriage to enable it to be towed by Mr Davies' car. As can be seen the wheels were detachable to enable it to be fired with its legs in the correct position.

The spigot mortar could be assembled on the base which has been preserved and will be resited in a suitable place on Elvetham Heath. The mortar was never fired from this base owing to the close proximity of the railway and the roads. A few practice firings were carried out at Dogmersfield Park using the method shown here. No. 1 Platoon with the spigot mortar were luckier than no. 5 Platoon with their Smith Gun, as they never received any ammunition.

CHAPTER NINETEEN

HOUSES & ROADS

The Holt. This large house was built for Dr Frere in the early years of the last century, and he lived there until his death just after the war. It stood in the Fleet Road midway between Birch Avenue and Westminster Close, on the opposite side of the road. An office block stands on the site today.
Dr Frere was a much-respected doctor who in later years held his surgery in his home. He was a great benefactor to the people of Fleet, and was involved with many organisations including the hospital.

Minley Road, looking up to the Station Bridge in about 1905 – at about the time when gas streetlights were introduced in Fleet. By this time most of the houses in this stretch of road had been built, and only three more were to be added. Just after 1980 the road junction on the left was closed as a new road and roundabouts had been built a few yards along the road.

These two wooden houses were built in Cove Road at the start of the 1900s when building restrictions were almost non-existent. The main timbers and the cladding were untreated softwood and by the time they were demolished in the late 1960s there were doubtless some structural problems. A pair of bungalows occupies the site today.

This wooden bungalow stood on the north side of Clarence Road close to Reading Road, and was built when the road was known as Middle Street in the last few years of the nineteenth century. It was not demolished until another bungalow had been built in the orchard on the left in the late 1940s. The wooden dwelling was then demolished and a brick bungalow was built on this site as well.

Great Bramshot Farmhouse, situated in the Cove Road close to Bramshot Bridge, was owned by the Watts family for almost all of the twentieth century. From the 1920s Rose Farm Dairy was run by farmer Mr Adams and dairyman Mr Cubby but when Mr Adams was killed in 1946 Mr Watts went into partnership with Mr Cubby. This arrangement continued until Mr Cubby retired, but Mr Watts continued to run the dairy until its demise in 1999. Milk production ceased on the farm in 1947.

The Oatsheaf crossroads, Crookham Road, with the hotel which was built in the 1850s on the right. The horse-trough provided drinking water for the many horses that would have passed through this area daily. The parade of shops along the Crookham Road is still much the same today. The crossroads have existed for hundreds of years: one arm, the Reading Road, was the main road from Farnham to Reading, and the other arm was the track from Crookham to the mill and on to Yateley and Bagshot.

Mr Voller's bakery. This was one of the early shops in Fleet Road and it stood on the north-west corner with Church Road. It was an attractive-looking building hung with rich red tiles. Mr Voller opened his bakery in the 1890s and remained here until the row of shops on the north-east corner of the junction was built in the 1920s. The business finally closed at the outbreak of the Second World War. The village pump was behind Mr Voller's first shop – there was no piped water at this time. To the left of this shop stood a fine old cottage, also dating to about 1890, with a large front garden but at the turn of the twentieth century Mr Barnwell built a lock-up shop in the garden for his cycle business. The old house remained until the mid-1980s when the site was redeveloped with offices over shops.

Pondtail Garage. Sited between Aldershot Road and Kings Road, this garage was opened in the late 1920s. The direction sign on the right gives a name that was commonly used at this time, although Hartley Row is now referred to as Wintney, the name for the whole area.

In 1924 Fleet UDC decided to build council houses to be let to deserving families. These six were built on the corner of Kings Road and Albany Road, and another three pairs were built in Elvetham Road. The houses pictured were demolished in 1970 and replaced by Albany Court, a complex for elderly people.

Boone Farmhouse was situated in the Crookham Road, just past the police station. Now called Stanton Lodge, it was one of the original farmhouses in Fleet. The farm covered the area of the Lea. Even in the 1950s you only had to walk just past the football ground to see cows, sheep and pigs. In 1888 Sir Arthur Sullivan rented this house while he wrote the music for the *Yeoman of the Guard*.

The first Fleet school, near All Saints'. In 1860 Fleet had a population of 300, about 30 or 40 of them being children. Mr Lefroy decided to buy a pair of newly built but unfinished cottages, which could be finished inside as required for the new school. Within five years the need for larger premises became obvious and the school in Albert Street was built. The first school was then converted to a house and is still occupied today.

Silver Jubilee decorations in Fleet Road in 1935, viewed from the Upper Street/Victoria Road junction looking towards the station. A block of shops and two floors of offices replaced the garden and notice-board in the 1960s.

Dinorben House had extensive grounds with some 119 acres between Reading Road and Coxheath Road bridges. The main lodge in Dinorben Avenue still stands and there was also a service lodge in Coxheath Road. The latter was demolished when Wickham Road was built. The last residents of the estate were the Chinnocks and the Gallsworthys, who lived there from 1872 till 1935 when the estate was sold off in lots. This picture shows the service lodge with Mr Hewitt the gamekeeper and his wife. His duties included looking after the game and taking care of the vermin as well as general duties. Just along the road stood the service lodge for Courtmoor House.

Reading Road bridge. The second bridge at this site had a hump-back, but after the war it was decided to build a new, realigned, bridge without a hump. After much furore the boating fraternity lost their case for more headroom and the County Council got their humpless bridge. Today boats have only about 5 feet 6 inches (water) headroom and pedestrians have to bend almost double to get under it!

Ferndale Road. At the end of the Second World War there was a desperate need for more houses, and one of the sites selected was the area of sandy scrubland bounded by the canal, Coxheath Road, Gally Hill Road, Aldershot Road and Reading Road. This was one of the first private developments leading from Gally Hill Road by the side of Crookham School through to the Verne where it joins Award Road. The landscape has changed greatly with nearly fifty years of shrub and tree growth.

Aldershot Road, Crookham, in the early 1920s. There were houses all the way from the crossroads to the War Department land, as well as a couple of shops, petrol pumps and two coal yards. A few yards behind the trees to the left was the clear sandy area where processions used to end during the war and fifty yards further on was Tweseldown racecourse, the army's steeplechase course. The flat course was on the Queen's Parade Ground at Aldershot.

William and Frank Jessett outside their shop in the 1930s, with their house on the left and the bakery, store and garages to the right. The store opened in the 1830s and when the railway came to Winchfield in 1843 mail was carried by rail instead of by road and a post office was established outside the station. Once the mail had been sorted it was quickly sent over to Jessett's, who ran the Crookham post office. The store was the only one for miles and it stocked food, clothes, hardware and much more. George Jessett took many photographs over the years of the various meetings on the green from the balcony above the shop.

Dogmersfield House was built on the site of one of the palaces belonging to the Bishops of Bath and Wells. Henry VI often stayed here and Catherine of Aragon met Henry VII and her future husband Prince Arthur here. An Elizabethan house is incorporated in the eighteenth-century mansion, and it was the Mildmays' home for many years.

Dogmersfield House had vast gardens, including this large eighteenth-century walled garden close by the house and stables. On either side of the entrance are two dovecotes: one is said to be the oldest in Hampshire and the other the most recent. The garden today is much the same as in this 1920s picture except that the feature at the end has been removed. About 300 yards in front of the house is a 20-acre lake with an abundance of water-birds.

Dogmersfield Church. The estate workers'
houses and the church stood between the
house and the lake but in 1800 Lady
Mildmay wished to have a better view of the
lake and so all the buildings were removed.
The church was rebuilt in 1806 in what was
eventually the farmyard close to the road and
a few years ago the whole site was in ruins,
but now all the buildings seem to have been
restored. This photograph shows the present
church near the Queens Head, which was
built in 1842. The bell tower housed four
bells which sadly remain silent today because
of structural problems, and there are
numerous memorials on the walls inside. A
sixteenth-century memorial to Anne Sutton
came from the original church, and there are
several from the second church.

Lord Mildmay's funeral. This was typical of the ritual observed over hundreds of years by the family of the 'squire',
who had his own private church and burial-ground. His coffin would be carried from house to church in the
horse-drawn farm wagon with the mourners walking behind. This was the funeral of the 6th Baronet, Sir Henry
St John Mildmay, who died on 14 April 1918. He was born on 28 April 1853, no doubt in Dogmersfield House.
Presumably he would be laid to rest in the vault of the second church.

Elvetham estate. The entrance to the estate today is along the Fleet–Hartley Wintney Road and the Hall has been a conference centre for the last forty-five years. Queen Elizabeth I visited Elvetham in 1591 and planted an oak tree to commemorate her visit – it is now more than 30 feet in circumference. An avenue of Wellingtonias just under a mile long was planted and the gardens reclaimed from 1963, as an ongoing project. A church has stood in the grounds since 1250 and the present St Andrew's, the former parish church of Elvetham, was rebuilt in 1840 by the 3rd Lord Calthorpe. It closed for services in 1969.

Opposite: The stable block at The Lea. The house, which later became Crookham House, was of sufficient size and importance to have a fine stable block at the rear. In 1861 Mr Lefroy built the house next to Crookham Church, opposite the Wyvern inn. After the war it was sold to North Hants Properties, who converted it into Crookham House Residential Hotel. It was demolished in the 1960s to make way for a housing estate.

Elvetham Hall. The first reference to a house on this site was dated 675 and the manor has been held by various families over the years. In 1535 Henry VIII was entertained here by John Seymour and later by his son Edward Seymour. The hall burnt down in 1849 and a white two-storeyed lodge was built on the site. This was added to in 1860 and developed into the present mansion by Lord Calthorpe. During the First World War it served as a hospital for wounded officers. The family lived in the house until after the Second World War. It was sold to ICI in 1953 and on to Lansing Bagnall in 1965. In the 1980s the managing director of Lansing Bagnall sold the Basingstoke factory to a German company, but kept the Hall.

Double Lodges, Minley Manor. This was one of several entrances to the manor, all of which had lodges. This one is on the Minley Road about half a mile from Fleet station. In the 1970s, when the nearby M3 was being constructed, the road passing the lodge was straightened and today the lodges are hardly visible from the new road. The lodges were built in the 1860s when the manor was rebuilt by the banker Raikes Currie. The manor itself is a slightly smaller version of the Château De Blois on the Loire. One of the main features of the estate is the 500 yard avenue of Wellingtonia and lime trees. The estate, some 2,500 acres, was purchased by the War Office in 1936 as a training area and is today used by the Royal Engineers.

ACKNOWLEDGEMENTS

I would like to thank the following individuals and organisations without whose assistance this book would not have been possible: Aldershot Military Museum, Mrs J. Aldridge, Mrs C. Ashcroft, Mrs A. Baldock, G. Barson, Mrs E. Beale, Mrs E. Bell, W. Boulter, Mrs J. Bowers, Mrs B. Brown, D. Brown, Mrs F. Butler, R. Byrne, J.P.B. Coles, Mrs G. Cousins, F. Crumplin, Mrs M. Fenwick, A. Fitzpatrick, Fleet & District Carnival Assoc., Mrs B. Fury, B. Gale, D. Gardner, Mrs J. Grace, Mrs D. Green, Mrs R. Hardy, R. Harrison, D. Hayes, Mrs C. Heathers, Mrs J. Hedger, I. Hester, S. Jones, R. Karn, Mrs J. Mardles, Mrs B. May, D. Millett, National Motor Museum, National Rifle Assoc., Mrs R. Peacock, Mrs J. Phillips, C. Powell, S. Purchase, M. Rich, Mrs M. Roe, Mrs S. Rowe, E. Short, Mrs D. Smith, Mrs E. Smith, A.W. Smithers, L. Southall, B. Stephens, D. Tapp, Mrs O. Tocock, Mrs J. Vincent, J. Welch, J. Woodman, Mrs O. Woodman and Mrs W. Wooley.

Although there are over 200 photographs in this book I am sure that there are many more tucked away in old cupboards or drawers somewhere in the area. I hope the publication of this volume encourages people to search out their old photographs – who knows, there might even be a third selection! It would be very sad if such items of interest were to be mistakenly consigned to the bin or a bonfire, and so lost forever.

While every effort has been made to establish copyright and permission sought to reproduce material where appropriate, the author and publisher apologise for any omissions, and will be happy to rectify these in any future edition.